LAURA ZAVAN

80 AUTHENTIC
ITALIAN SWEET
TREATS, CAKES
& DESSERTS

PHOTOGRAPHY BY AKIKO IDA

MURDOCH BOOKS

80 AUTHENTIC ITALIAN SWEET TREATS, CAKES & DESSERTS

TABLE OF CONTENTS

INTRODUCTION

As far back as I can remember, I have always associated desserts with family gatherings. *Pandoro* and *panettone* at Christmas time, *focaccia* at Easter and *zuppa inglese* during the holidays at my Aunt Vige's house.

My travels to all corners of "sweet Italy" have led me to discover other wonders: all of them are revealed here in this book, a sort of map of the sweet and delicate! The *cannolo* with ricotta will transport you to Sicily, the *pastiera* to Naples, the *pandolce* to the coast of Liguria…

Here, these recipes from the Italian tradition are made simpler, lighter, easy to make and still delicious. There is a secret to this: it lies in the choice and quality of ingredients, including sugar and flour, without forgetting a generous dose of love when making the dish and just a dash of moderation when it comes to eating it!

Italian *dolci* are, above all else, about family and simplicity. They are a tradition that, for a long time, was passed down only by word of mouth. Historically, their presence has been more prominent in the wealthier northern regions, and in Sicily and Campania, where their ingredients were more readily available.

Each region has its signature ingredients. In the north, it is cow's milk (mascarpone, butter and cream), grains (corn, rice and buckwheat), hazelnuts and chestnuts, and fruit (apples and berries). In the south, it is ricotta, nuts (almonds and pistachios), fruit (figs and candied fruits), wheat and olive oil.

A little history

Cakes and biscuits grew out of bread-making, and were created to celebrate an event, usually a religious one. Thus, *il pan* (bread) became *pandolce* (sweet bread), *pan d'oro* or *pandoro* (golden bread), and so on. The practice of baking them developed in the monasteries and convents, where the raw materials — honey, flour, eggs, milk, and so on — were on hand.

It was only after 1000AD that cane sugar and spices such as vanilla, saffron and cinnamon arrived, thanks to the first crusades and Venetian traders. The 14th century marked the beginning of more elaborate pâtisserie. The Renaissance paid tribute to sugar and Venice led the way. In his book *Opera dell'arte del cucinare* (printed in Venice in 1570), Bartolomeo Scappi, a cook in the service of Pope Pius V, compiled a veritable bible of recipes in which sugar is omnipresent. As symbols of wealth and markers of social status, the use of expensive sugar and priceless spices allowed the aristocracy to set itself apart from the lower classes.

The real pâtisserie revolution took place in the 19th century, with the beginnings of sugar beet cultivation and the democratisation of sugar!

TIRAMISÙ
&
CO

THE 'OFFICIAL' TIRAMISÙ FROM MY TOWN

It was in Treviso, my home town in the region of Veneto, that tiramisù was born.
At the end of the 1960s, the restaurant Le Beccherie baptised this dessert
"Tirami sù" ("pick me up" in English) because the combination of eggs, sugar and
coffee is an excellent... pick-me-up! This unusual name has contributed to its fame.
The original recipe was given to me by Signor Campeol, owner of Le Beccherie.

20 minutes preparation time
2 hours refrigeration time
Serves 8–10

6 egg yolks
140 g (5 oz/⅔ cup) raw (demerara) sugar
500 g (1 lb 2 oz) mascarpone cheese
250 g (9 oz) ladyfinger biscuits or
   30–40 *savoiardi (see page 116)*
300 ml (10½ fl oz) strong espresso coffee, lukewarm
2 tablespoons unsweetened cocoa powder

Whisk the egg yolks and sugar in a large bowl until the mixture
has a mousse-like consistency. Mix in the mascarpone to make
a smooth cream.

Dip the biscuits briefly in the coffee, then arrange them in a large round serving
dish (the original shape of the genuine tiramisù) or a stainless steel ring. Spread
half the mascarpone cream over the layer of biscuits. Cover with a second
layer of biscuits dipped in coffee, then another layer of mascarpone cream.

Refrigerate for at least 2 hours before serving. When ready to serve, dust the
tiramisù with the cocoa powder using a small sieve. Eat within 24 hours.

To pasteurise the egg yolks
*To keep your tiramisù for up to 3 days, heat the sugar in a saucepan with
40 ml (1¼ fl oz) water. When the syrup reaches 120°C (235°C), pour it in a thin
stream into the whisked yolks and keep whisking until the mixture cools down.
Mix in the mascarpone, then proceed as per the recipe.*

PAVESINI® TIRAMISÙ

Pavesini® are the biscuits of my childhood. Light, with a unique taste, you will find them in Italian grocery shops or delicatessens in their unchanged yellow packaging. The addition of alcohol is optional, but I recommend Marsala *fine*, meaning 'dry'.

30 minutes preparation time
2 hours refrigeration time
Serves 8–10

5 eggs, separated
100 g (3½ oz) raw (demerara) sugar
500 g (1 lb 2 oz) mascarpone cheese
50 ml (1¾ fl oz) dry (*fine*) Marsala (optional)
300 ml (10½ fl oz) strong espresso coffee, lukewarm
1 packet Pavesini® (8 sachets)
2 tablespoons unsweetened cocoa powder

Whisk the egg yolks with 60 g (2¼ oz) of the sugar in a large bowl until the mixture has a mousse-like consistency. In a separate bowl, whisk the egg whites with the remaining sugar until stiff peaks form. Mix the mascarpone into the yolk–sugar mixture, then gently fold in the whisked egg whites, turning the mixture up from the base of the bowl.

If using the Marsala, add it to the coffee. Dip the Pavesini® biscuits briefly into the lukewarm coffee. The biscuits should be moistened but not soaked. In a deep serving dish, arrange a layer of biscuits and cover with a third of the mascarpone cream. Repeat this process twice.

Refrigerate for at least 2 hours before serving. When ready to serve, dust the tiramisù with the cocoa powder using a small sieve. Eat within 24 hours.

Tiramisù with whipped cream
For a creamier tiramisù, replace the egg whites with 200 g (7 oz) whipped cream (unsweetened) and beat all of the 100 g (3½ oz) sugar directly with the egg yolks.

BERRY TIRAMISŪ

Delizioso when the strawberry season begins! But if you don't have the patience
to wait for the strawberries and raspberries, you can make this dish with
a simple coulis of fresh or frozen berries.

30 minutes preparation time
2 hours refrigeration time
Serves 8–10

5 eggs, separated
100 g (3½ oz) raw (demerara) sugar
500 g (1 lb 2 oz) mascarpone cheese
250 g (9 oz) ladyfinger biscuits or
  30–40 *savoiardi (see page 116)*
50 g (1¾ oz/⅓ cup) strawberries, hulled and halved
125 g (4½ oz/1 cup) raspberries
125 g (4½ oz) blueberries

For the coulis
250 g (9 oz/1⅔ cups) strawberries, hulled
40 g (1½ oz) sugar
juice of 1–2 oranges

Whisk the egg yolks and 60 g (2¼ oz) of the sugar in a large bowl
until the mixture has a mousse-like consistency. In a separate bowl,
whisk the egg whites with the remaining sugar until firm. Mix the
mascarpone into the yolk-sugar mixture, then gently fold in the whisked egg
whites, turning the mixture up from the base of the bowl.

To make the coulis, purée the strawberries in a food proocessor with the sugar
(adjusting the amount of sugar depending on how sweet the strawberries are)
and the orange juice. Strain the coulis to remove the seeds.

Spread a little mascarpone cream around the base of a deep serving dish. Dip
half of the biscuits into the coulis to moisten them well and arrange them in the
dish. Pour half the mascarpone cream over the biscuits. Repeat this process, then
arrange the halved strawberries on top with the raspberries and blueberries.

Refrigerate for at least 2 hours before serving.

ROSE & RASPBERRY TIRAMISÙ

Here is a variation on the mascarpone cream usually used in tiramisù — a light, rose-scented sabayon. Very girly! It's made here with pretty *Roses de Reims* biscuits, a French biscuit coloured pink with cochineal, but ladyfingers are an ideal substitute.

20 minutes preparation time
10 minutes cooking time
2 hours refrigeration time
Makes 6 glasses

250 g (9 oz) mascarpone cheese
50 ml (1¾ fl oz) rose syrup
100 ml (3½ fl oz) thickened (whipping) cream
12 ladyfinger biscuits or *savoiardi (see page 116)*
100 ml (3½ fl oz) rosewater
200 g (7 oz) raspberries, to decorate

For the sabayon
3 egg yolks
50 g (1¾ oz) raw (demerara) sugar
100 ml (3½ fl oz) rosewater

To make the sabayon, beat the egg yolks in a large bowl with the sugar and rosewater. Place the bowl on top of a saucepan of simmering (not boiling) water, making sure the base of the bowl does not touch the water, and beat for about 10 minutes using an electric beater, until the mixture has a mousse-like consistency. Let the mixture cool, stirring from time to time.

Combine the mascarpone with the rose syrup, then gently fold the mixture into the sabayon. In a separate bowl, whip the cream and add it to the sabayon mixture.

Place 2 tablespoons of sabayon cream in each serving glass. Moisten the biscuits with the rosewater and place them on top (about 2 biscuits per glass). Cover with more sabayon cream.

Refrigerate for at least 2 hours before serving. Decorate with the raspberries before serving.

QUICK TIRAMISÙ

This is my express recipe for when friends drop in. This tiramisù is made without eggs, using ingredients you'd find in a local corner shop. It can even be served after a lightning-quick half hour in the freezer instead of the usual 2 hours in the refrigerator.

20 minutes preparation time
2 hours refrigeration time, or 30 minutes freezing time
Makes 6 glasses

200 ml (7 fl oz) strong espresso coffee, lukewarm
60 ml (2 fl oz/¼ cup) dry (*fine*) Marsala (or other alcohol)
250 g (9 oz) mascarpone cheese
60 g (2¼ oz/½ cup) icing (confectioners') sugar
1 sachet (7.5 g/¼ oz) vanilla sugar
200 ml (7 fl oz) thin (pouring) cream, well chilled
24 ladyfinger biscuits or *savoiardi (see page 116)*
100 g (3½ oz) good dark chocolate, grated, or
   2 tablespoons unsweetened cocoa powder

Pour the coffee into a shallow bowl and add 20 ml (½ fl oz) of the Marsala. In a separate bowl, using a whisk or a wooden spoon, beat the mascarpone with the icing sugar, vanilla sugar and the remaining Marsala. Once the mixture is quite smooth, add the cream, little by little, beating with a whisk.

Dip half the biscuits in the coffee before arranging them in serving glasses. Cover with half the mascarpone mixture, then sprinkle with the chocolate or dust with cocoa powder. Repeat this process.

Refrigerate for at least 2 hours before serving, or 30 minutes in the freezer.

Substitutes for the mascarpone
You can replace the mascarpone with crème fraîche or fromage blanc (fresh curd cheese). If you use fromage blanc, whip the cream before folding it in.

AMARETTI TIRAMISÙ

I adore *amaretti*! These typically Italian biscuits with their bitter almond flavour
are like macaroons, and give an extraordinary twist to this tiramisù.
You can make them yourself — it's very easy.

20 minutes preparation time
2 hours refrigeration time
Makes 6 small glasses

3 eggs, separated
60 g (2¼ oz) sugar
250 g (9 oz) mascarpone cheese
2 tablespoons dry (*fine*) Marsala (optional)
9 soft *amaretti* (*see page 108*)
200 ml (7 fl oz) strong espresso coffee, lukewarm
2 tablespoons unsweetened cocoa powder

Whisk the egg yolks and 40 g (1½ oz) of the sugar in a large bowl
until the mixture become mousse-like in consistency. Add the
mascarpone and whisk until you have a thick cream. Mix in the
Marsala (if using). In a separate bowl, beat the egg whites with the remaining
sugar until firm. Gently fold this mixture into the mascarpone cream.

Dip the *amaretti* in the coffee, flattening them a little. In each glass, place
1 tablespoon of mascarpone cream and half an *amaretto*. Cover with
mascarpone cream to the top of the glass, then push a whole *amaretto*
into the middle.

Refrigerate for at least 2 hours before serving. Just before serving, dust the
tiramisù with the cocoa powder using a small sieve.

Quality amaretti
*At Italian grocery shops or delicatessens you will find soft amaretti from Sassello
(Liguria) and crunchy amaretti from Saronno (Lombardy), as well as local
versions. You can also try my recipe on page 108.*

LIMONCELLO TIRAMISÙ

The Sorrento Peninsula, next to Naples, is famous for its lemons, which are used to make *limoncello*. This liqueur is poured over ice before drinking (in moderation!), or used for soaking *babà* — mushroom-shaped sponge cakes, another local speciality.

15 minutes preparation time
30 minutes refrigeration time
Makes 6 small glasses

3 eggs, separated
60 g (2¼ oz) raw (demerara) sugar
250 g (9 oz) mascarpone cheese
1 x 300 g (10½ oz) jar of mini *babà* in *limoncello (see note below)*
finely grated zest of 1 lemon (preferably unwaxed), to decorate

Whisk the egg yolks in a large bowl with 40 g (1½ oz) of the sugar until the mixture is a mousse-like consistency. Mix in the mascarpone, whisking until a thick cream forms. Add a few spoonfuls of the *babà* syrup, to taste.

In a separate bowl, beat the egg whites with the remaining sugar until firm. Fold this mixture gently into the mascarpone cream.

Fill each serving glass three-quarters full with the mascarpone cream, top with a small *babà* and decorate with the lemon zest.

Refrigerate for at least 30 minutes before serving.

Babà in limoncello
You will find jars of mini babà in limoncello in Italian grocery shops or delicatessens. If you can't find them, replace them with ladyfinger biscuits dipped in limoncello diluted with a little water.

RICOTTA CREAM WITH STRAWBERRIES & LEMON

This is an ultra-light recipe, without any eggs or biscuits, and the mascarpone is replaced with ricotta. The lemon zest adds even more freshness to this summery dessert. I always use organic citrus fruits, which I find are not as bitter and have more flavour.

15 minutes preparation time
2 hours refrigeration time
Makes 4–6 glasses

500 g (1 lb 2 oz) sheep's milk ricotta
170 g (6 oz) icing (confectioners') sugar
½ teaspoon vanilla powder
finely grated zest of 1 lemon (preferably unwaxed)
250 g (9 oz/1⅔ cups) strawberries, plus 4–6 extra, for decoration
2 tablespoons chopped, unsalted pistachio nuts, for decoration

For the coulis
250 g (9 oz/1⅔ cups) strawberries, hulled
50 g (1¾ oz) raw (demerara) sugar
a few drops of lemon juice

For the coulis, purée the strawberries with the sugar and a few drops of lemon juice. Strain to remove the seeds.

Push the ricotta through a sieve into a large bowl. Sift together the icing sugar and vanilla powder then stir this, and the lemon zest, into the ricotta.

Hull and dice the strawberries and divide them between the serving glasses. Cover with the coulis, then the ricotta cream. Halve the extra strawberries and place on top with a sprinkling of chopped pistachios.

Refrigerate for at least 30 minutes before serving.

The different types of ricotta
There are different types of ricotta — it's up to you to find out what's best at your local delicatessen. Sheep's milk and buffalo milk ricottas are, in principle, tastier and creamier than cow's milk ricotta, but may be harder to find. Try tracking them down from artisan producers at local farmers' or growers' markets.

ZUPPA INGLESE

I love this spoon dessert, made from liqueur-soaked genoise sponge cake and crème pâtissière. *Zuppa inglese*, literally "English soup", is typical of the Emilia-Romagna region (my Aunt Vige was a specialist!) and the neighbouring region of Tuscany. It might have originated from the English trifle.

40 minutes preparation time
3–4 hours refrigeration time
40 minutes cooking time
Serves 8

250 g (9 oz) genoise *(see pan di spagna, page 149)*, or
   200 g (7 oz) ladyfinger biscuits or *savoiardi (see page 116)*
1 quantity crème pâtissière *(see page 151)*
80 g (2¾ oz) dark chocolate (70% cocoa)
200 ml (7 fl oz) *alchermes* liqueur or rum *(see note below)*
3 tablespoons *amarene* (sour cherries) in syrup (optional)

Make the genoise, preferably the day before. Make the crème pâtissière and divide it between two bowls. Melt the chocolate in a double boiler (or a heatproof bowl over a saucepan of hot water, making sure the hot water doesn't touch the base of the bowl). Mix the melted chocolate with one of the bowls of crème pâtissière.

Line an 18–20 cm (7–8 inch) mixing bowl with plastic wrap. In a small bowl, dilute the *alchermes* with 200 ml (7 fl oz) of water and use this to moisten the genoise. Gently press out any excess liquid with your hands.

Cut the genoise into 1.5 cm (⅝ inch) thick rectangular strips and arrange these close together and side by side over the base and side of the lined bowl. Pour the plain crème pâtissière over this genoise base and smooth the surface well. Halve the *amarene* cherries and arrange them on top of the crème. Cover with a layer of genoise, then the chocolate crème pâtissière. Top with a final layer of genoise.

Cover with plastic wrap and refrigerate for at least 3 hours. Unmould onto a plate before serving.

Alchermes liqueur
Alchermes is a bright red, sweet and spicy liqueur. Its name is derived from the Arabic quirmiz (cochineal), used to colour it. The original recipe is based on spices (cinnamon, cloves, nutmeg, vanilla), aromatic herbs and flowers (rose and jasmine). You can find it in specialist liquor shops.

PANNA
COTTA
&
CO

MY VANILLA PANNA COTTA

In Italian, *panna cotta* means "cooked cream". This dish, inspired by custards but without any eggs, was born about a century ago in the Piedmont region. I like to serve this simple panna cotta with a berry coulis and a few raspberries. The combination of the cream with the acidity of the fruit is so good!

15 minutes preparation time
7 minutes cooking time
2 hours refrigeration time
Makes 4 small glasses

500 ml (17 fl oz/2 cups) thickened (whipping) cream
1 vanilla bean, split lengthways and seeds scraped
finely grated zest of ½ lemon (preferably unwaxed)
40 g (1½ oz) sugar
1 teaspoon agar-agar (*see note on page 32*)
1 tablespoon cornflour (cornstarch)

For about 200 ml (7 fl oz) coulis
250 g (9 oz/1⅔ cups) strawberries, hulled, or raspberries
30–40 g (1–1½ oz) sugar, or to taste
a few drops of lemon juice, to taste

Heat 400 ml (14 fl oz) of the cream with the vanilla bean and seeds and the lemon zest in a saucepan over a low heat. Add the sugar once the cream is warm.

In a small bowl, combine the agar-agar with the cornflour and blend this mixture with the remaining cream. Add this mixture to the warm cream, whisking to avoid lumps forming. Bring to the boil, stirring all the time. Take the saucepan off the heat and allow the mixture to cool until just warm, stirring regularly.

Remove the vanilla bean and divide the cream between four serving glasses. Let the mixture cool to room temperature. Cover with plastic wrap and refrigerate for at least 2 hours to set.

For the coulis, purée the fruit in a food processor with the sugar and lemon juice to taste, then strain to remove the seeds. Thin out the consistency with a little water if necessary. Pour a layer of coulis on top of the panna cottas to serve.

Other coulis ideas
All summer fruits (peaches, apricots, mangoes, passionfruit, cherries) and berries (blackberries, blueberries) will be wonderful because their tart flavour will contrast with the creaminess of the panna cotta. Out of season, use low-sugar jams, thinned with a little water.

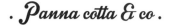
. *Panna cotta & co* .

COFFEE PANNA COTTA

The coffee–lemon pairing is a souvenir of a drink enjoyed in the Apulia region in summer: *caffè in ghiaccio,* an espresso poured over a glass of ice cubes with an aromatic twist of lemon peel. I love rediscovering the flavours of this very refreshing iced coffee in my panna cotta.

20 minutes preparation time
7 minutes cooking time
2 hours refrigeration time
Makes 4–5 glasses

500 ml (17 fl oz/2 cups) thickened (whipping) cream
10 g (¼ oz) instant coffee granules
finely grated zest of 1 lemon (preferably unwaxed)
1 vanilla bean, split lengthways and seeds scraped
50 g (1¾ oz) sugar
1 teaspoon agar-agar (*see note on page 32*)
1 tablespoon cornflour (cornstarch)
good-quality dark chocolate shavings, to decorate
tuile-style biscuits or ladyfinger biscuits
   or *savoiardi (see page 116)*, to serve

Place 400 ml (14 fl oz) of the cream, the coffee blended into a very small amount of water, the lemon zest and the vanilla bean and seeds in a saucepan over a low heat.

Once the cream is warm, add the sugar. In a small bowl, combine the agar-agar with the cornflour and blend this mixture with the remaining cream. Combine this mixture with the warm cream, whisking to avoid lumps forming. Bring the mixture to the boil, continuing to stir.

Take the pan off the heat and let the mixture cool down until just warm, stirring regularly. Pour the cream into serving glasses and let it cool to room temperature. Cover with plastic wrap and refrigerate for at least 2 hours for the cream to set before serving.

Decorate with shavings of chocolate and serve chilled with a few biscuits.

Caffeine-free chicory panna cotta
You can replace the coffee with 6 rounded tablespoons of instant chicory.

LICORICE PANNA COTTA

Licorice gives this dish a mild and pleasant bitterness, in addition to its digestive properties. The best pure licorice comes from Calabria, extracted from the roots of a plant that has been cultivated there since the Middle Ages. You will find it in Italian grocery or confectionery shops, sold as hard pastilles in pretty little Amarelli-brand tins.

15 minutes preparation time
7 minutes cooking time
2 hours refrigeration time
Makes 4–5 glasses

500 ml (17 fl oz/2 cups) thickened (whipping) cream
8 g (¼ oz) pure licorice pieces
40 g (1½ oz) sugar
1 teaspoon agar-agar (*see note below*)
1 tablespoon cornflour (cornstarch)

Pour 400 ml (14 fl oz) of the cream over the pieces of licorice in a saucepan (crush the licorice if needed so it dissolves more quickly). Heat over a low heat, stirring constantly, until the licorice has completely dissolved, then turn off the heat and allow to cool until just warm. Add the sugar.

In a small bowl, combine the agar-agar with the cornflour and blend this mixture into the remaining cream. Mix this mixture into the licorice cream in the saucepan, whisking to avoid lumps forming. Bring to the boil over a low heat, continuing to stir. Take the saucepan off the heat and let the mixture cool a little, stirring regularly.

Pour the cream into serving glasses and let the mixture cool to room temperature. Cover with plastic wrap and refrigerate for at least 2 hours before serving. Serve chilled.

A plant-based setting agent
I use agar-agar in my panna cotta recipes, mixed with cornflour for a smoother texture. Agar-agar, a red algae extract, melts at 80°C (175°F) and starts to set at 25°C (75°F).

If you don't have it, you can replace the agar-agar/cornflour mixture with 4–5 g (⅛ oz) gelatine (which is an animal product) for 500 ml (17 fl oz/ 2 cups) cream.

CHOCOLATE PANNA COTTA

Make this dessert with a very good dark couverture chocolate with a cocoa content of 60–70%. It melts beautifully and its flavours are intense. You will find it in chocolate or speciality shops.

20 minutes preparation time
7 minutes cooking time
4 hours refrigeration time, or overnight
Serves 6–8

250 g (9 oz) good-quality dark chocolate (60–70% cocoa, preferably couverture)
500 ml (17 fl oz/2 cups) thickened (whipping) cream
500 ml (17 fl oz/2 cups) milk
80 g (2¾ oz) sugar
2 teaspoons agar-agar *(see note on page 32)*
1 tablespoon cornflour (cornstarch)

Finely chop the chocolate with a knife. In a saucepan, heat 400 ml (14 fl oz) of the cream with the milk over a low heat, then add the sugar. In a small bowl, combine the agar-agar with the cornflour and blend into the remaining cream. Combine this mixture with the cream in the saucepan, whisking to avoid lumps forming. Bring to the boil, continuing to stir.

Take the saucepan off the heat and allow the mixture to cool until just warm, stirring regularly. Add the chocolate and stir with a wooden spoon until it has completely melted.

Rinse a large 18 cm (7 inch) silicone mould under water and don't wipe it dry, this will make it easier to unmould the panna cotta later. Pour the cream mixture into the mould and let it cool to room temperature.

Cover with plastic wrap, then refrigerate for at least 4 hours (or, even better, overnight). Unmould onto a plate and serve chilled.

White chocolate panna cotta
Use 200 g (7 oz) white chocolate instead of the dark chocolate and leave out the sugar.

BITTER ALMOND
PANNA COTTA

Almonds are the veritable economic and gastronomic lifeblood of Sicily.
To recreate the fine almond flavours of the island, I took inspiration from the
Sicilian *biancomangiare** and *gelo**. I wanted to create a creamier version
of these traditional almond-based dishes.

20 minutes preparation time
7 minutes cooking time
2–4 hours refrigeration time, or overnight
Serves 4–6

350 ml (12 fl oz) thickened (whipping) cream
40 g (1½ oz) sugar
1 teaspoon agar-agar (*see note on page 32*)
1 tablespoon cornflour (cornstarch)
150 ml (5 fl oz) unsweetened almond milk
40 ml (1¼ fl oz/2 tablespoons) bitter almond extract
    (use according to strength)
80 g (2¾ oz/4 tablespoons) bitter orange marmalade, to serve

Pour the cream into a saucepan over a low heat and add the sugar.
In a small bowl, combine the agar-agar with the cornflour and blend with
the almond milk. Add this mixture to the cream in the saucepan, whisking
to avoid lumps forming.

Bring the cream mixture to the boil, continuing to stir. Take the saucepan off
the heat and let the mixture cool a little, stirring regularly. Add a little bitter
almond extract, taste and adjust by adding more if needed.

Rinse 4–6 small individual moulds (without wiping them dry to make it easier
to unmould the panna cottas later), then pour the cream into the moulds.
Let the mixture cool to room temperature. Refrigerate for 2–4 hours (or, even better,
overnight), for the cream to set.

Unmould and serve the panna cottas with orange marmalade, thinned out
with a little water, or simply plain.

**Biancomangiare is a completely white almond-based cream that dates back
hundreds of years, while gelo is a refreshing and summery dish typical of Sicily.
It is made from a sweet liquid (almond milk, watermelon juice, melon juice,
lemon juice) gelled with cornflour.*

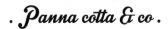

POMEGRANATE & ORANGE FLOWER PANNA COTTA

The flavours of the Mediterranean inspire this panna cotta, delicately perfumed with orange flower water. Delicious! Orange flower water is made by distilling the flowers of the bitter orange tree, the essence of which is called *neroli*. Try to buy some from a good grocery shop. Avoid artificial flavours.

20 minutes preparation time
7 minutes cooking time
2–4 hours refrigeration time, or overnight
Serves 4–6

350 ml (12 fl oz) thickened (whipping) cream
40 g (1½ oz) sugar
1 teaspoon agar-agar *(see note on page 32)*
1 tablespoon cornflour (cornstarch)
150 ml (5 fl oz) milk
40 ml (1¼ fl oz) orange flower water
1 pomegranate

Heat the cream in a saucepan over a low heat and add the sugar. In a small bowl, combine the agar-agar with the cornflour and blend with the milk. Stir this mixture into the cream in the saucepan, whisking to avoid lumps forming. Bring to the boil, continuing to stir. Take the saucepan off the heat, add the orange flower water and allow the mixture to cool until just warm, stirring regularly.

Quarter the pomegranate. Take out the seeds and soak them in a bowl of water: the white, hard-to-remove membrane will rise to the surface. Set aside half of the prettiest seeds for decoration and the other half to go into the panna cottas.

Rinse 4–6 small individual moulds (without wiping them dry, to make it easier to unmould the panna cottas later). Divide the pomegranate seeds for the panna cottas between the moulds, then fill with the lukewarm cream. Let the mixture cool to room temperature.

Refrigerate for 2–4 hours (or, even better, overnight), for the cream to set. Unmould and decorate with the reserved pomegranate seeds.

. *Panna cotta & co* .

PISTACHIO & SOUR CHERRY PANNA COTTA

A very delicious and surprising panna cotta: the unique flavour of pistachio goes wonderfully with the smoothness of the cream and the tart note of the preserved *amarene* (sour cherries). Try making it with Sicilian pistachio paste.

30 minutes preparation time
7 minutes cooking time
2–4 hours refrigeration time, or overnight
Serves 4–6

500 ml (17 fl oz/2 cups) thickened (whipping) cream
40 g (1½ oz) sugar
1 teaspoon agar-agar *(see note on page 32)*
1 tablespoon cornflour (cornstarch)
50 g (1¾ oz) unsweetened pistachio paste (from health food or Italian grocery shops)
1 tablespoon unsalted pistachio nuts, to decorate
2 tablespoons sour cherries in syrup, to decorate

Pour 400 ml (14 fl oz) of the cream into a saucepan over a low heat and add the sugar. In a small bowl, combine the agar-agar with the cornflour and blend this mixture into the remaining cream. Add this mixture to the cream in the saucepan, whisking to avoid lumps forming. Bring to the boil, continuing to stir.

Remove the saucepan from the heat, then add the pistachio paste to the cream mixture and stir well to blend it in completely. Allow this mixture to cool until just warm, stirring regularly.

Rinse 4–6 small individual moulds (without wiping them dry, to make it easier to unmould the panna cottas later). Pour the mixture into the moulds. Let the moulds cool to room temperature, then refrigerate for 2–4 hours (or, even better, overnight), for the cream to set.

Unmould and serve decorated with pieces of pistachio and a few cherries.

Bronte pistachios
The pistachio originated in the Middle East and spread through Italy by the Arabs from the 10th century onwards. It found its ideal terrain in Bronte in Sicily, at the foot of Mount Etna in the soils fertilised by the ashes of the volcano. Bronte pistachios are considered to be the best for their flavour and nutritional qualities. They are more expensive because they are harvested from the hilly lava fields entirely by hand.

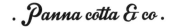

AMARETTI CUSTARD
BONET

Bonet is a delicious amaretti custard typical of the Piedmont region. Its name suggests the colour and shape of an old-fashioned bonnet or the copper mould it used to be cooked in. There is also an older version of *bonet* in the Monferrato region that doesn't contain any cocoa powder or chocolate.

20 minutes preparation time
45–75 minutes cooking time
3 hours refrigeration time, or overnight
Serves 6

100 g (3½ oz) crunchy *amaretti* biscuits
500 ml (17 fl oz/2 cups) milk
4 eggs, at room temperature
130 g (4¾ oz) caster (superfine) sugar
40 ml (1¼ fl oz) strong espresso coffee
40 ml (1¼ fl oz) rum
40 g (1½ oz/⅓ cup) unsweetened cocoa powder

Preheat the oven to 160°C (315°F). Using a food processor, grind the *amaretti* to a fine powder. Put the milk in a saucepan and warm over a low heat.

In a bowl, beat the eggs with 80 g (2¾ oz) of the sugar, then mix in the ground *amaretti*, coffee, rum, cocoa powder and lukewarm milk. Gently whisk without frothing the mixture, to avoid small air bubbles forming during cooking.

Make a caramel using the remaining sugar: moisten the sugar with 1 tablespoon of water in a saucepan over a low heat and cook until it is a deep, golden colour. Coat the bases and sides of six small moulds or one 18 cm (7 inch) mould with a thin layer of caramel. Let the caramel cool a little before pouring in the custard mixture.

Place the moulds in a container filled with boiling water reaching almost to the top of the sides. Bake the custards for 45 minutes for the small moulds or 1 hour and 15 minutes for the large one. The custards should be set but still wobble a little in the middle.

Let them cool and refrigerate for at least 3 hours (or, even better, overnight). Pass a knife blade around the custards and unmould onto plates to serve.

ROAST FIGS & MASCARPONE CREAM

A ripe fig is the ultimate indulgence; the soft, yielding flesh has a honey-like sweetness. Figs have two seasons: a quick, short burst in early summer and a second, main crop that begins in late summer and runs through autumn. With names like the black Genoa and white Adriatic, they practically sing of Italy! Make the most of an abundance of figs by making this delicious dessert.

10 minutes preparation time
20 minutes cooking time
Serves 6

24 figs, ripe but firm
25 g (1 oz) butter, plus extra, for greasing
2 tablespoons acacia honey
50 ml (1¾ fl oz) dry (*fine*) Marsala
a few rosemary sprigs
1 quantity mascarpone cream *(see page 152)*

Preheat the oven to 180°C (350°F), fan-forced. Wash the figs briefly, remove their stems and cut them almost into quarters, leaving them attached at the base. Arrange the figs in a large buttered baking dish.

Pour the honey and Marsala over the figs in a thin stream, add the rosemary sprigs and dot with small pieces of butter. Bake for 20 minutes, basting regularly with the cooking juices. Serve the figs just warm with their juices, accompanied by the mascarpone cream.

Variation with apricots
Halve the apricots and remove their stones. Follow the recipe above but cook at 200°C (400°F) under the oven grill, for 8–10 minutes. You can also replace the mascarpone cream with ricotta cream (see page 22, paragraph 2 of method).

AMARETTI-STUFFED PEACHES

This very old dessert is supposed to be Piedmontese in origin. Some recipes replace the cocoa powder in the filling with cinnamon or candied fruits. The famous Artusi, in his book *La scienza in cucina e l'arte di mangiar bene* (1891), replaces the *amaretti* with *savoiardi* (ladyfingers). Here, I give you my favourite version of this recipe.

20 minutes preparation time
20 minutes cooking time
Serves 6

6 large yellow peaches, just ripe
180 g (6½ oz) soft *amaretti* (*see page 108*)
1 egg yolk
1 heaped tablespoon unsweetened cocoa powder
30 g (1 oz) butter, plus extra, for greasing
200 ml (7 fl oz) Muscat wine, or 100 ml (3½ fl oz) dry (*fine*) Marsala
    diluted with 100 ml (3½ fl oz) water
2 tablespoons icing (confectioners') sugar, for dusting

ash the peaches. Cut them in two without removing their skin, remove their stones and hollow them out just a little using a small spoon. Save the scooped-out flesh.

Preheat the oven to 180°C (350°F).

Combine the *amaretti*, egg yolk, cocoa powder and scooped-out peach flesh in a food processor and pulse until the mixture is smooth.

Grease a baking dish and arrange the peaches in it, cut side up. Fill each halved peach with 2 teaspoonfuls of stuffing and place a thin slice of butter on each.

Sprinkle with the sweet wine and bake for 10 minutes. Spoon all of the cooking juices over the peaches and cook for a further 10 minutes.

Serve warm or cold, dusted with icing sugar.

ITALIAN MONT BLANC
MONTE BIANCO

Dedicated to the highest mountain in Europe, this decadent dessert is made from cooked chestnuts and chantilly cream. It is supposed to have originated in France, though it is very popular in the Piedmont, Lombardy and Veneto regions. The Italian Mont Blanc is often served as a dome of sweet chestnut purée (like a mountain) topped with chantilly cream.

30 minutes preparation time
6 hours refrigeration time
Serves 5–6

350 ml (12 fl oz) thickened (whipping) cream
40 g (1½ oz/⅓ cup) icing (confectioners') sugar
about 15 small meringues, crumbled into small pieces
3–4 whole chestnuts in syrup (or *marrons glacés*)

For the chestnut 'vermicelli'
200 g (7 oz) unsweetened chestnut purée
180 g (6½ oz) *crème de marrons* (sweetened chestnut purée)
1 pinch vanilla powder
20 g (¾ oz) icing (confectioners') sugar, sifted, or to taste
1 teaspoon rum
50 g (1¾ oz) butter, melted

Whip the cream with the icing sugar in a bowl. Set aside 100 g (3½ oz) of the whipped cream and refrigerate until required. Mix the remaining whipped cream with the crumbled meringues. Spoon the cream–meringue mixture into individual 8 cm (3¼ inch) moulds lined with plastic wrap and freeze for at least 6 hours, or until set.

For the chestnut vermicelli, place the unsweetened chestnut purée in a bowl and use a wooden spoon to loosen it. Combine it with the *crème de marrons*. Add the vanilla powder, icing sugar, rum and cooled butter. Taste and add more sugar if needed. Pour the chestnut mixture into a piping bag fitted with a Mont Blanc nozzle (which produces thin, vermicelli-like strands) or a small fluted nozzle.

Break each chestnut into two or three pieces. Unmould the frozen creams onto serving plates and pipe over the chestnut vermicelli in spirals, from the bottom to the top. Decorate with the reserved chantilly cream and pieces of chestnut. Serve immediately.

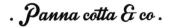

TARTS
&
TARTLETS

GRANDMOTHER'S TART
TORTA DELLA NONNA

Liguria and Tuscany both claim ownership of this dessert, found everywhere in the *trattorie* and bars of northern Italy. This tart is perfect for a comforting treat. The combination of shortcrust pastry, crème pâtissière and pine nuts is to die for!

40 minutes preparation time
40 minutes cooking time
2 hours 30 minutes refrigeration time
20 minutes resting time
Serves 6–8

1 quantity shortcrust pastry (*see page 148*)
1 quantity crème pâtissière (*see page 151*)
100 g (3½ oz/⅔ cup) pine nuts (preferably Italian) (*see tip*)

Make the shortcrust pastry according to the recipe on page 148. Leave the pastry dough to rest in the refrigerator for 2 hours, then remove it and leave for 20 minutes at room temperature.

Grease a loose-based 24 cm (9½ inch) round tart tin. Roll out the pastry about 3 mm (⅛ inch) thick on a lightly floured work surface. Line the tin with the pastry and trim the excess using a sharp knife. Prick the base with a fork and return it to the refrigerator for at least 30 minutes.

Preheat the oven to 180°C (350°F).

Make the crème pâtissière according to the recipe on page 151. Pour the cold crème pâtissière into the tart shell and smooth the surface with the back of a spoon. Scatter over the pine nuts and bake for about 40 minutes, or until the top is golden.

Tip
Soak the pine nuts in water for 5 minutes before scattering them on the tart so they don't brown too quickly during cooking.

MASCARPONE & BERRY TARTLETS

Inspired by the classic *crostata di frutta* (fruit tart), these tartlets combine the smooth flavour of the mascarpone cream with the freshness of raspberries and blueberries. Delicious! In springtime, you can replace these berries with strawberries.

40 minutes preparation time
30 minutes cooking time
2 hours 30 minutes refrigeration time
20 minutes resting time
Makes 6 tartlets, or 1 large tart

1 quantity shortcrust pastry *(see page 148)*
1 egg white, beaten, for brushing the pastry

For the filling
1 quantity mascarpone cream *(see page 152)*
finely grated zest of 1 lemon (preferably unwaxed)
250 g (9 oz/2 cups) raspberries
250 g (9 oz) blueberries
2 tablespoons ground pistachio nuts

Make the shortcrust pastry according to the recipe on page 148. Leave the pastry dough to rest in the refrigerator for 2 hours, then remove it and leave for 20 minutes at room temperature. Roll it out on a lightly floured work surface until it's about 3 mm (⅛ inch) thick.

Grease six individual 8 cm (3¼ inch) square tartlet tins, or one large tart tin. Line with the pastry and trim the excess. Refrigerate for at least 30 minutes.

Preheat the oven to 170°C (325°F).

Make the mascarpone cream according to the recipe on page 152, adding the finely grated lemon zest at the same time as the sugar and vanilla seeds. Refrigerate until required.

Prick the base of the pastry cases with a fork and cover with a sheet of baking paper weighted with baking beads or dried beans, to stop it puffing up. Bake for 20 minutes, then remove the paper and beads and bake for a further 5 minutes. To avoid the pastry absorbing moisture from the filling, brush the base with the egg white and return to the oven for 2 minutes. Allow to cool.

Fill the baked tart cases with the mascarpone cream and arrange the raspberries and blueberries on top. Before serving, sprinkle with the ground pistachios.

LEMON & ALMOND CROSTATA

Here is a tart that conjures up the south of Italy. As for any simple dish, the quality of the ingredients is crucial: in Italy, the best lemons come from the Amalfi (Campania) and Syracuse (Sicily) coasts. Choose firm, preferably organic lemons, unwaxed if possible.

✦

30 minutes preparation time
35 minutes cooking time
2 hours 30 minutes refrigeration time
20 minutes resting time
Serves 6–8

1 quantity shortcrust pastry *(see page 148)*

For the filling
5 eggs
140 g (5 oz/⅔ cup) raw (demerara) sugar
90 g (3¼ oz) butter, melted
3 lemons (preferably unwaxed)
100 g (3½ oz) almonds, flaked or roughly chopped
50 g (1¾ oz) icing (confectioners') sugar

Make the shortcrust pastry according to the recipe on page 148. Leave the pastry dough to rest in the refrigerator for 2 hours, then remove it and leave for 20 minutes at room temperature. Roll it out on a lightly floured work surface until it's about 3 mm (⅛ inch) thick.

Grease a 35 x 10 cm (14 x 4 inch) loose-based rectangular tart tin. Line it with the pastry and trim the excess using a sharp knife. Refrigerate for at least 30 minutes.

Preheat the oven to 180°C (350°F).

Beat the eggs and sugar in a large bowl. Add the melted butter and the finely grated zest and juice of 2 lemons. Prick the base of the tart with a fork and scatter over the flaked almonds. Pour in the lemon mixture and dust over 40 g (1½ oz/⅓ cup) of the icing sugar.

Bake for about 25 minutes, until golden. Slice the last lemon into rounds and dust with the remaining icing sugar. Arrange the rounds on top of the tart and bake for a further 10 minutes.

RICOTTA TART WITH DRIED FRUIT
TORTA ALLA RICOTTA CON FRUTTA SECCA

Ricotta is a dairy product, not a cheese. Its name comes from "ri-cotta", which means that the whey — a by-product of cheese-making — is cooked twice. Ricotta dates back to Roman times, and each region in Italy uses it in different ways.

40 minutes preparation time
40–60 minutes cooking time
2 hours 30 minutes refrigeration time
20 minutes resting time
Serves 8

1 quantity shortcrust pastry *(see page 148)*

For the filling
50 g (1¾ oz) raisins
1 small glass (approximately 55 ml/1¾ fl oz) dry
   (fine) Marsala or rum
500 g (1 lb 2 oz) ricotta (preferably
   sheep's milk)
2 eggs
100 g (3½ oz) raw (demerara) sugar
40 g (1½ oz) butter, melted
1 teaspoon ground cinnamon
finely grated zest of 1 lemon
   (preferably unwaxed)
50 g (1¾ oz) candied citron, diced

Make the shortcrust pastry according to the recipe on page 148. Leave the pastry dough to rest in the refrigerator for 2 hours, then remove it and leave for 20 minutes at room temperature. Roll it out on a lightly floured work surface.

Grease one 22 cm (8½ inch) loose-based tart tin. Line with pastry and trim the excess with a sharp knife, keeping a 1 cm (½ inch) overhang. Prick the base with a fork. Refrigerate for at least 30 minutes.

Preheat the oven to 160°C (315°F).

In a small bowl, soak the raisins in the Marsala. In a large bowl, work the ricotta with a spatula until it is smooth. Add the eggs, sugar, melted butter, cinnamon, lemon zest, citron, the soaked raisins and the Marsala they were soaked in. Pour the mixture into the tin.

Bake for about 1 hour for one large tart, or 40 minutes for tartlets, until golden.

Variations
Each region in Italy has its own recipe for ricotta tart. My aunt from Reggio Emilia used to make it with anise liqueur. In the south of Italy, they use orange flower water.

. Tarts & tartlets .

WHEAT, RICOTTA & ORANGE FLOWER TARTS
PASTIERA NAPOLITANA

Pastiera is found on every Neapolitan table on Easter Sunday (though it is eaten all year round today). It dates back to pagan festivals in Rome celebrating the return of spring, with ingredients such as eggs, symbolising rebirth, or wheat and ricotta, symbolising prosperity. You'll find whole wheat or spelt grains in health food shops.

50 minutes preparation time
2 hours refrigeration time
20 minutes resting time
50-75 minutes cooking time
Makes 6–8 tartlets

1 quantity shortcrust pastry *(see page 148)*

For the filling
200 g (7 oz) whole wheat or spelt
200 ml (7 fl oz) milk
200 g (7 oz) sugar
2 eggs
300 g (10½ oz) ricotta (preferably sheep's milk)
finely grated zest of 1 lemon (preferably unwaxed)
1 pinch ground cinnamon
50 g (1¾ oz) candied citron, diced
50 g (1¾ oz) candied orange, diced
40 ml (1¼ fl oz) orange flower water, or to taste

Place the wheat in a saucepan with 400 ml (14 fl oz) of water. Bring to the boil and cook for 20–45 minutes, or until the wheat is *al dente*. Drain. Meanwhile, make the shortcrust pastry according to the recipe on page 148 and refrigerate it for 2 hours.

Combine the cooked wheat with the milk and 30 g (1 oz) of the sugar in a saucepan over a low heat. Simmer until the milk is almost completely absorbed and the wheat is tender. Allow to cool.

In a large bowl, beat together the eggs and the remaining sugar. Whisk in the ricotta, lemon zest and cinnamon. Add the milk-wheat mixture, the candied citrus fruits and the orange flower water.

Remove the pastry from the refrigerator and leave to rest for 20 minutes at room temperature. Roll it out on a lightly floured work surface to around a 3 mm (⅛ inch) thickness.

Preheat the oven to 180°C (350°F). Meanwhile, grease six to eight 8 cm (3¼ inch) tartlet tins and line with the pastry, trimming the overhang with a sharp knife. Prick the bases with a fork and fill with the wheat-ricotta filling. Make strips from the pastry offcuts and lay them on top of the filling in a cross shape.

Bake for 30 minutes, or until the tartlets are golden brown.

. Tarts & tartlets .

ALMOND CRUMB BISCUITS
FREGOLOTTA

In Veneto, *fregola* means "crumb". This homely biscuit is effectively made from crumbs of shortcrust pastry. It crumbles if you cut it with a knife, so it is recommended that you break it into pieces by hand. It can be enjoyed with a coffee, a glass of sweet wine or, for the more decadent, some mascarpone cream.

15 minutes preparation time
30–40 minutes cooking time
1 hour refrigeration time
Serves 6

100 g (3½ oz) blanched almonds
200 g (7 oz/1⅓ cups) plain (all-purpose) flour,
    plus extra, for the tartlet tins
100 g (3½ oz) raw (demerara) sugar, plus extra,
    for sprinkling
2 pinches salt
finely grated zest of 1 lemon (preferably unwaxed)
1 pinch vanilla powder
100 g (3½ oz) chilled butter, cut into pieces, plus
    extra, for greasing
2 small egg yolks

To serve
1 quantity mascarpone cream *(see page 152)*

Set aside 12 or so whole almonds for decoration and roughly chop the rest. Using your fingertips, combine the flour in a bowl with the sugar, salt, lemon zest, vanilla, butter, chopped almonds and egg yolks. The mixture should be crumbly, made up of hazelnut-sized pieces. Don't work the dough for too long.

Grease and flour six 8 cm (3¼ inch) tartlet tins, or one large tart tin. Fill them with mixture, pressing lightly with your fingers. Refrigerate for 1 hour.

Preheat the oven to 160°C (315°F).

Lightly press the whole almonds into the dough and sprinkle with a little sugar. Bake the tartlets for about 30 minutes, or 40 minutes for one large tart, until golden.

Enjoy the *fregolotte* at room temperature, preferably the next day, with the mascarpone cream and small glasses of *passito* or other sweet wine.

CAKES
&
FESTIVE
CAKES

CHOCOLATE AMARETTI CAKE

My favourite chocolate cake is enriched with the hint of almond flavour that's the signature of amaretti. I never get tired of it! If you use rice flour instead of wheat flour, you will have a gluten-free cake.

30 minutes preparation time
25 minutes cooking time
Serves 6–8

100 g (3½ oz) dark dessert chocolate (60–70% cocoa)
100 g (3½ oz) butter, plus 20 g (¾ oz), for greasing
70 g (2½ oz) crunchy *amaretti* (or soft *amaretti, see page 108*)
3 eggs
150 g (5½ oz) raw (demerara) sugar
50 g (1¾ oz/⅓ cup) plain (all-purpose) flour (or rice flour)
1 teaspoon baking powder (preferably organic)

For the icing
100 g (3½ oz) dark dessert chocolate (60–70% cocoa)
100 ml (3½ fl oz) thin (pouring) cream
70 g (2½ oz/⅔ cup) toasted flaked almonds or crumbled *amaretti*

Melt the chocolate with the butter in a double boiler (or a heatproof bowl over a saucepan of hot water, making sure the hot water doesn't touch the base of the bowl). Stir regularly.

Preheat the oven to 180°C (350°F).

Generously grease a 22–24 cm (8½–9½ inch) round cake tin with the remaining butter. Grind the crunchy *amaretti* in a food processor, then coat the base and side of the tin with them (or crumble soft *amaretti* directly into the greased tin). Set aside in the refrigerator.

Beat the eggs and sugar using an electric beater. Once the mixture has a mousse-like consistency, gently fold in the flour and baking powder, then the melted and cooled chocolate.

Pour the batter into the cake tin and bake for 25 minutes, or until a skewer inserted in the centre comes out clean. Let the cake cool in the tin before turning it out onto a wire rack.

For the icing, melt the chocolate and cream in a double boiler (or a heatproof bowl over hot water, as above). Mix together well. Pour the icing onto the cake, spreading it with a flexible spatula. Scatter over the toasted flaked almonds or crumbled *amaretti*.

. Cakes & festive cakes .

APPLE & AMARETTI CAKE

My apple cake recipe is inspired by the one made by my great friend Betty's mother, Fioretta. The *amaretti* and dry Marsala give it a unique flavour.

30 minutes preparation time
1 hour cooking time
Serves 6–8

1 kg (2 lb 4 oz) golden delicious apples
2 eggs
120 g (4¼ oz) raw (demerara) sugar
20 ml (½ fl oz) dry (*fine*) Marsala
250 ml (9 fl oz/1 cup) thin (pouring) cream
finely grated zest of 1 lemon (preferably unwaxed)
150 g (5½ oz/1 cup) plain (all-purpose) flour
3 teaspoons baking powder (preferably organic)
1 pinch fine salt
60 g (2¼ oz) crunchy *amaretti*

Peel the apples and cut them into thin slices. Set aside around 20 slices for decoration. In a large bowl, lightly beat the eggs with the sugar. Add the Marsala, cream and lemon zest, then the flour, sifted with the baking powder and salt. Mix the apples into this batter.

Preheat the oven to 180°C (350°F) and line a 22–24 cm (8½–9½ inch) round springform cake tin with baking paper.

Finely grind the *amaretti* in a food processor or with a rolling pin. Cover the base of the tin with half of the ground *amaretti*. Mix the rest of the ground *amaretti* into the batter before pouring it into the tin.

Arrange the reserved apple slices on top in a rosette pattern, pressing them gently onto the surface of the cake. Bake for 1 hour, or until golden. Serve warm or at room temperature.

RICOTTA RING CAKE
CIAMBELLA ALLA RICOTTA

This easy-to-make cake is a little like a yoghurt cake. It is enjoyed at breakfast time,
or as an afternoon snack. The texture can vary depending on the type of ricotta:
if it is too dry, add a little cream to loosen the mixture. Each region and each
family has its own version of *ciambella*.

30 minutes preparation time
20 minutes soaking time
40 minutes cooking time
Serves 6–8

60 g (2¼ oz/⅓ cup) raisins
1 small glass (approximately 55 ml/1¾ fl oz) anise-flavoured
   liqueur or rum
3 eggs
200 g (7 oz) raw (demerara) sugar
250 g (9 oz) ricotta
150 g (5½ oz/1 cup) butter, melted and cooled,
   plus 10 g (¼ oz) extra, for greasing
150 g (5½ oz) plain (all-purpose) flour, plus
   extra, for coating
100 g (3½ oz) potato starch
1 teaspoon baking powder (preferably organic)
40 g (1½ oz/¼ cup) pine nuts or pistachio nuts

Preheat the oven to 180°C (350°F). In a small bowl, soak the raisins in the
alcohol for 20 minutes. In a large bowl, beat the eggs with the sugar until
the mixture is pale and light and has doubled in volume. Mix in the ricotta,
then the butter, beating continuously.

Sift together the flour, potato starch and baking powder and gradually add
them to the mixture, stirring to combine well. Drain the raisins, reserving the
alcohol they were soaked in. Coat the raisins in a little flour (this will stop them
from sinking to the base of the tin), then add to the mixture with the pine nuts
and 40 ml (1¼ fl oz) of the reserved alcohol.

Grease a 24–26 cm (9½–10½ inch) ring tin, pour in the cake batter and bake
for 40 minutes, or until golden. Serve warm or at room temperature.

PEAR & CHESTNUT MILLEFOGLIE

This is a version of the French pastry mille-feuille (literally "a thousand leaves" in both French and Italian) that uses tuile biscuits instead of puff pastry — much simpler to make! Thank you to Manuela, my dear friend, for the inspiration. I make the tuiles, crème pâtissière and fruit in advance and put the dessert together at the last minute. You can use other fruit according to the season, such as berries, figs or peaches.

≡

45 minutes preparation time
20 minutes cooking time
Serves 8

4 large williams pears
2 knobs butter
2 tablespoons raw (demerara) sugar
1 jar of chestnuts in syrup
icing (confectioners') sugar, for dusting

1 quantity crème pâtissière (see page 151)

For the tuiles
4 egg whites, at room temperature
125 g (4½ oz/1 cup) icing (confectioners') sugar
175 g (6 oz) plain (all-purpose) flour
200 g (7 oz) butter, melted and cooled

Preheat the oven to 180°C (350°F) fan-forced. Make the crème pâtissière according to the recipe on page 151. Set it aside in a mixing bowl until it has cooled, covered with plastic wrap in direct contact with the surface of the crème.

To make the tuiles, whisk the egg whites in a bowl with the sifted icing sugar. Add the sifted flour and cooled butter.

Place 1 tablespoon portions of the mixture in well-spaced mounds on a baking tray covered with baking paper (for 24 tuiles, allow about three trays). Spread each mound out thinly, using the back of a spoon, to make discs about 10 cm (4 inches) in diameter. Bake for 10–15 minutes, or until just coloured.

Meanwhile, peel the pears and cut them into small cubes. Cook the cubes in a frying pan with the butter and sugar for 5 minutes. Allow to cool.

Drain and roughly chop 5 or 6 chestnuts. To assemble the dish just before serving: place a tuile on each plate, top with a generous spoonful of crème pâtissière, then a spoonful of pear, and scatter over a few pieces of chestnut. Repeat this process two more times. Dust with icing sugar and serve immediately.

SANDY CAKE
TORTA SABBIOSA

This vanilla-flavoured cake, very popular in Veneto, is said to have been invented in Pavia (Lombardy) at the end of the 19th century. The texture, made using potato starch and icing sugar, is reminiscent of fine sand (*sabbia* in Italian). Beyond Veneto, it is more commonly known as *torta paradiso*. It is a quite substantial cake, more an afternoon snack than a dessert.

40 minutes preparation time
40 minutes cooking time
Serves 6–8

200 g (7 oz) butter, softened, plus extra,
    for greasing
½ vanilla bean
200 g (7 oz) icing (confectioners') sugar,
    plus extra, for dusting
3 eggs, lightly whisked, at room temperature
100 g (3½ oz/⅔ cup) plain (all-purpose) flour,
    plus extra, for the cake tin
100 g (3½ oz) potato flour (potato starch)
1 pinch fine salt

Have the butter at room temperature for at least 3 hours ahead of time. Preheat the oven to 170°C (325°F).

Scrape out the seeds of the vanilla bean half. In a large bowl, beat the softened butter with the icing sugar and vanilla seeds until creamy. Add the whisked eggs, one spoonful at a time, mixing well after each addition until you have a thick and smooth consistency.

Sift the flour and potato starch together before gradually incorporating them into the mixture. Add the salt and mix through.

Grease and flour a 22–24 cm (8½–9½ inch) round cake tin. Pour in the batter and bake for 40 minutes, or until golden. Cool in the tin for 1 hour, then remove and dust with icing sugar before serving.

AUNT VIGE'S RICE CAKE
TORTA DI RISO

My Aunt Vige used to make this delicious anise-scented rice cake. This rustic cake, dating back to the 19th century, originated in Reggio Emilia and Modena. The recipe is surely connected to the rice harvests in the Po Valley.

20 minutes preparation time
55 minutes cooking time
Serves 6–8

1 litre (35 fl oz/4 cups) milk
1 pinch salt
150 g (5½ oz) short-grain rice such as Arborio
   (preferably risotto rice)
butter and flour, for greasing and dusting
150 g (5½ oz) raw (demerara) sugar
120 ml (4 fl oz) anise-flavoured liqueur, or
   dry (*fine*) Marsala
finely grated zest of 1 lemon (preferably unwaxed)
3 eggs, separated
1 tablespoon icing (confectioners') sugar,
   for dusting

Bring the milk to the boil in a saucepan with a pinch of salt. Add the rice, stir and cook for 8 minutes, or until *al dente*. Allow to cool until just warm.

Preheat the oven to 180°C (350°F). Grease and flour a 25 x 20 cm (10 x 8 inch) rectangular cake tin. Once the rice is lukewarm, add the sugar, 80 ml (2½ fl oz/ ⅓ cup) of the liqueur, the lemon zest and the egg yolks, one by one, stirring after each addition, then the lightly whisked egg whites. Mix together well.

Using a slotted spoon, fill the tin with the rice mixture, then pour over any liquid still in the saucepan. Bake for 45 minutes, until browned.

When the cake comes out of the oven, dust it with icing sugar and drizzle with the remaining liqueur. Serve warm or at room temperature.

HAZELNUT & BUCKWHEAT CAKES

These little cakes are the take-away version of a larger cake typical of the Trentino–Alto Adige region, made from buckwheat flour and toasted hazelnuts and served topped with redcurrant jam. Not to be missed!

≡

40 minutes preparation time
55–65 minutes cooking time
Serves 6–8

180 g (6½ oz) whole blanched hazelnuts
170 g (6 oz) butter, softened, plus extra,
   for greasing
150 g (5½ oz) raw (demerara) sugar
1 pinch fine salt
1 teaspoon ground cinnamon
4 eggs
190 g (6¾ oz) buckwheat flour (see note),
   plus extra, for the tin
½ teaspoon baking powder (preferably organic)
redcurrant or berry jam, to serve

Have the butter at room temperature for at least 3 hours ahead of time. Preheat the oven to 180°C (350°F). Grease and flour a 6- or 8-hole muffin tin or one large 22–24 cm (8½–9½ inch) round cake tin.

Spread the hazelnuts on a baking tray and toast in the oven for about 15 minutes, turning every 5 minutes, until they are golden. Let the hazelnuts cool, then finely grind them in a food processor.

In a large bowl, work the softened butter with 70 g (2½ oz) of the sugar, the salt and cinnamon until creamy. Lightly beat 2 whole eggs with 2 egg yolks, incorporating them little by little into the butter mixture. Mix well after each addition, using a spatula or wooden spoon, until the consistency is thick and smooth.

In a clean bowl, whisk the 2 egg whites with the remaining sugar until firm. Sift the flour with the baking powder and mix into the batter with the ground hazelnuts. Add the whisked egg whites.

Divide the mixture into the muffin tin, or pour it into the cake tin. Bake for 40 minutes for the small cakes or 50 minutes for the large one. Serve warm or at room temperature, with your choice of jam.

Note
Buckwheat has been grown in the Alpine valleys of northern Italy since the middle of the 16th century. In the Valtellina and Trentino–Alto Adige regions, its naturally gluten-free flour is used in savoury dishes.

. Cakes & festive cakes .

CHOCOLATE ALMOND CAKE
TORTA CAPRESE

This gluten-free cake, typical of the Sorrento peninsula and Amalfi coast, takes its name from the island of Capri. It's said to have been created in the 1920s by a pastry chef who forgot to add the flour to his cake batter.

40 minutes preparation time
40 minutes cooking time
Serves 6–8

250 g (9 oz) blanched almonds
180 g (6½ oz) raw (demerara) sugar, plus
  2–3 teaspoons extra, for the ground almonds
250 g (9 oz) dark chocolate (60–70% cocoa)
200 g (7 oz) butter, softened, plus extra, for greasing
5 eggs, separated, at room temperature
1 pinch fine salt
icing (confectioners') sugar, for dusting

Preheat the oven to 180°C (350°F). Spread the almonds on a baking tray and toast in the oven for 10 minutes, then allow to cool. Coarsely grind them using a coffee grinder or in a food processor. Add 2–3 teaspoons of sugar, to taste.

Melt the chocolate in a double boiler (or a heatproof bowl over a saucepan of hot water, making sure the hot water doesn't touch the base of the bowl). Let the chocolate cool until just warm.

Using an electric stand mixer or a wooden spoon, beat the softened butter in a bowl with 100 g (3½ oz) of the sugar until very creamy. Add the egg yolks one at a time, mixing well after each addition. Add the ground almonds and salt. Pour the chocolate into the mixture little by little and gently combine.

In a clean bowl, beat the egg whites to soft peaks with the remaining sugar to make a smooth meringue. Using a spatula, gently fold it into the chocolate mixture, making sure not to collapse the meringue.

Grease a 22–24 cm (8½–9½ inch) round cake tin and line with baking paper. Pour in the batter and bake for about 40 minutes. Remove from the tin to cool and dust with icing sugar before serving.

Blanching almonds
If you are using unblanched almonds, drop them into boiling water for a few minutes, off the heat. Squeeze them gently to remove the skin. You can also soak them overnight in water at room temperature.

. Cakes & festive cakes .

ORANGE CREAM SPONGE CAKE
GENOISE A L'ORANGE

A genoise is a classic Italian sponge cake, the foundation of many Italian and French sweets. This delicious cake is filled with orange-flavoured crème anglaise — I love its delicate flavour and melting texture. Interestingly, the Italians call a genoise sponge *pan di spagna* ("Spanish bread"), while the French associate it with the city of Genoa.

1 hour preparation time
50 minutes cooking time
2 hours refrigeration time
Serves 6–8

1 genoise (*pan di spagna*) *(see page 149)*
1 quantity crème anglaise *(see page 150)*

2 oranges (preferably unwaxed)
50 g (1¾ oz) caster (superfine) sugar
20 ml (½ fl oz) orange-flavoured liqueur
3 tablespoons bitter orange marmalade
120 g (4¼ oz/¾ cup) blanched almonds
300 ml (10½ fl oz) thin (pouring) cream
30 g (1 oz) icing (confectioners') sugar

Make the genoise the day before according to the recipe on page 149. Use a 26 cm (10½ inch) round cake tin and, once cooked, cut the cake into three horizontal layers with a bread knife. The next day, make the crème anglaise as per the recipe on page 150.

In a saucepan over a medium–high heat, bring the juice and grated zest of 1 orange to the boil with the sugar. When the juice starts to caramelise, add the liqueur and marmalade, and continue cooking for 3 minutes. Cool the mixture to just warm and mix into the crème anglaise.

Line a 26 cm (10½ inch) round cake tin with plastic wrap. Place one disc of genoise in the base of the tin and spread evenly with a third of the orange crème anglaise. Repeat this process twice. Refrigerate the cake for at least 2 hours.

Toast the almonds for 10 minutes at 180°C (350°F), then chop them with a knife. Remove the cake from the tin.

In a bowl, whip the cream with the icing sugar. Spread two thirds of it around the side of the cake and press the almonds around the side. Place the cake on a serving plate, decorate with the remaining whipped cream and threads of orange zest from the second orange.

. Cakes & festive cakes .

SICILIAN CREAM CAKE
CASSATA SICILIANA

Cassata is a very well known Sicilian cake. Originally a cake for Easter and springtime — the best season for ricotta — it is now found all year round in the *pasticceria*. I love this slightly over-the-top dessert, loaded with colours and flavours, which is nevertheless easy to make. You'll find green marzipan at specialist cake-decorating shops, or try mixing plain marzipan with a few drops of green food colouring.

1 hour preparation time
35 minutes cooking time
2 hours refrigeration time
Serves 8

1 genoise (*pan di spagna*)
    (*see page 149*)

For the filling
600 g (1 lb 5 oz) ricotta (preferably
    sheep's milk)
100 g (3½ oz) icing (confectioners') sugar
1 pinch vanilla powder
70 g (2½ oz) candied citron or orange,
    diced
70 g (2½ oz) dark chocolate (60–70%
    cocoa), chopped
150 g (5½ oz) green marzipan
70 ml (2¼ fl oz) dry (*fine*) Marsala
    diluted with 70 ml (2¼ fl oz) water

For the decoration
1 egg white
150 g (5½ oz) icing (confectioners') sugar
20 ml (½ fl oz) lemon juice
300 g (10½ oz) candied fruit, whole
    or in quarters (citron, orange,
    lemon, melon)

Make the genoise according to the recipe on page 149. Cut into rectangular strips 1.5 cm (⅝ inch) thick. Push the ricotta through a sieve, into a large bowl, then mix it with the sifted icing sugar, vanilla, diced candied fruit and chopped dark chocolate.

Line a 22–24 cm (8½–9½ inch) round cake tin with plastic wrap. Roll out the marzipan to about a 2 mm (¹⁄₁₆ inch) thickness and cut a strip the same height as the side of the tin. Lay this strip around the inside of the tin. Arrange rectangles of genoise side by side in the base of the tin and brush them with the diluted Marsala to moisten. Cover with the ricotta cream, even out the surface with a spoon and cover with more strips of genoise brushed with Marsala.

Cover the cassata with plastic wrap and place a weight on top, then refrigerate for at least 2 hours. Unmould onto a serving plate.

Before serving, whisk the egg white in a bowl with the icing sugar and lemon juice. Spread this icing over the cassata. Decorate with wafer-thin slices of candied fruit, sliced using a mandoline or a knife.

MY BIRTHDAY CAKE

I decorate this cake with whatever takes my fancy at the time — edible flowers, sweets, sugar flowers, berries. You can replace the Marsala with your favourite liqueur. Happy Birthday!

1 hour preparation time
30 minutes resting time
50 minutes cooking time
Serves 8

1 genoise *(pan di spagna) (see page 149)*
1 pinch vanilla powder
1 quantity crème pâtissière *(see page 151)*
80 g (2¾ oz) dark chocolate (60–70% cocoa)
500 ml (17 fl oz/2 cups) thickened (whipping) cream,
    well chilled
2 tablespoons icing (confectioners') sugar
300 ml (10½ fl oz) dry *(fine)* Marsala diluted
    with 100 ml (3½ fl oz) water

For the decoration
your choice of edible flowers, coloured
    sweets, berries

Make the genoise according to the recipe on page 149, adding the pinch of vanilla powder when you add the flour and salt. Make the crème pâtissière as per the recipe on page 151. While it is still warm, combine half the crème pâtissière with the chocolate, chopped into small pieces.

Whip the cream in a bowl with the icing sugar. Fold a third of the whipped cream into the chocolate crème pâtissière, another third into the plain crème pâtissière and set aside the rest for decoration.

Slice the genoise into three horizontal layers using a bread knife and brush them with the diluted Marsala to moisten. Spread the plain crème pâtissière on the first round of cake, cover with the second round, spread over the chocolate crème pâtissière and top with the third round.

Top the cake with whipped cream and decorate as desired.

PANETTONE CHRISTMAS LOG

The Venetian tradition of enjoying slices of *panettone* spread with mascarpone and *mostarda* (candied fruit with mustard oil) at Christmas time gave me the idea for this very easy Christmas log. The slight bite of the *mostarda* gives a wonderful lift to the creaminess of the mascarpone.

===

40 minutes preparation time
2 hours refrigeration time, or overnight
Serves 6–8

1 x 380 g (13½ oz) jar *mostarda Veneta* (from
    Italian grocery shops)
500 g (1 lb 2 oz) mascarpone cheese
400 ml (14 fl oz) thickened (whipping) cream, chilled
1 artisanal *panettone*, 500 g (1 lb 2 oz)
100 ml (3½ fl oz) dry (*fine*) Marsala (or sweet white
    wine) diluted with 100 ml (3½ fl oz) water

Purée three-quarters of the *mostarda* in a food processor. Chop the remainder into a small dice. In a large bowl, work the mascarpone with a spatula until it is smooth and creamy and add the *mostarda* purée. In a separate bowl, whip the cream and fold it gently into the mascarpone mixture.

Line a 32 cm (12¼ inch) long loaf (bar) tin with plastic wrap, with enough overhanging at each side to cover when the log is assembled. Cut the *panettone* into 1.5 cm (⅝ inch) slices and line the tin with them. Brush the slices of panettone with the diluted Marsala to moisten. Pour over a third of the mascarpone mixture. Repeat this process and finish with a layer of *panettone*.

Cover the log with the overhanging plastic wrap, place a weight on top and refrigerate it for at least 2 hours or, even better, even overnight. Unmould the log onto a plate, cover each side with the remainimg mascarpone cream and decorate with the diced *mostarda*.

Panettone
Panettone is THE Italian Christmas cake! Originating in Milan, it can be found on every Italian table during the festive season (outside of this period, you rarely see it on sale). Choose a traditional artisanal panettone, which you will find in Italian grocery shops, delicatessens and some supermarkets.

DECADENT PANDORO CAKE

Pandoro is, with *panettone*, a classic Italian Christmas dessert. This star-shaped brioche, vanilla-scented and rich in butter, is originally from Verona. Created in the mid-19th century, it's said to have evolved from the *nadalin*, the Venetian *pan de oro*, or even the *Kugelhupf* that the Austrians brought to Veneto. This ultra-decadent version, decorated like a little Christmas tree, is perfect for impressing your guests during the festive season.

—

30 minutes preparation time
Serves 10

3 egg yolks, at room temperature
50 g (1¾ oz) raw (demerara) sugar
40 ml (1¼ fl oz) of your choice of alcohol such as rum,
    dry *(fine)* Marsala or amaretto, or the seeds of 1 vanilla bean
250 g (9 oz) mascarpone cheese
250 ml (9 fl oz/1 cup) thin (pouring) cream, well chilled
1 artisanal *pandoro*, 1 kg (2 lb 4 oz)
seeds from 1 pomegranate, or 100 g (3½ oz) redcurrants
2 tablespoons icing (confectioners') sugar, for dusting

Beat the egg yolks in a large bowl with the sugar and alcohol or vanilla seeds, until the mixture is pale and light. Add the mascarpone and whisk until it becomes thick and creamy. In a separate bowl, whip the cream and fold it gently into the mascarpone mixture.

Cut the *pandoro* into horizontal slices about 2 cm (¾ inch) thick. Cut the widest slices into two or three pieces.

To serve, reassemble the *pandoro* in a star shape. Using a spatula or piping (icing) bag, spread the slices with mascarpone cream and scatter with the pomegranate seeds, then stack them on top of each other.

Decorate with the remaining pomegranate seeds. Using a sieve, dust the cake with icing sugar.

Tip
You can slice the pandoro ahead of time: place the slices back in its plastic packaging so it doesn't dry out and fill with the cream mixture at the last moment. You can also serve the pandoro sliced into star shapes with the filling on the side.

GENOESE PANDOLCE WITH DRIED FRUIT

Pandolce is a Christmas treat in Genoa and Liguria. The oldest version is the pandolce alto (high pandolce), which uses a sourdough base. It takes longer to prepare than the pandolce basso, made with baking powder. Thanks to Annalisa for her family recipe.

=

30 minutes preparation time
10 minutes soaking time
20 minutes refrigeration time
40 minutes cooking time
Makes 8–10 serves, or 1 large *pandolce*

210 g (7½ oz) raisins
80 g (2¾ oz) butter, softened
100 g (3½ oz) raw (demerara) sugar
1 pinch vanilla powder
1 pinch fine salt
2 teaspoons fennel seeds
1 egg
20 g (¾ oz) pine nuts
50 g (1¾ oz) candied orange, diced
50 g (1¾ oz) candied citron, diced
300 g (10½ oz/2 cups) plain (all-purpose) flour
½ sachet (3.5 g/⅛ oz) baking powder (preferably organic)
80 ml (2½ fl oz/⅓ cup) milk
40 ml (1¼ fl oz) rum

Soak the raisins in a small bowl of lukewarm water for 10 minutes. In a large bowl, cream the softened butter well with the sugar and vanilla. Add the salt and fennel seeds then, still mixing, add the egg, drained raisins, pine nuts and diced candied fruit.

Sift the flour with the baking powder and add it to the mixture with the milk and rum. Briefly knead by hand, or use an electric stand mixer, until it forms a ball. Make sure the pine nuts and candied fruits are evenly distributed throughout the mixture but don't overwork it.

Place the ball of dough on a baking tray lined with baking paper and flatten it into a circle about 4 cm (1½ inches) thick.

Preheat the oven to 180°C (350°F).

Using the back of a knife or a plastic spatula, lightly score a lattice pattern on the surface of the dough. Leave to rest for 20 minutes in the refrigerator, then bake for about 40 minutes, or until golden brown.

Long shelf-life
Pandolce is better eaten the day after making and keeps improving from there. It will keep, wrapped in plastic wrap, for up to 20 days.

. *Cakes & festive cakes* .

POLENTA CAKE WITH DRIED FRUIT
PINZA

This rustic and very filling dessert is an Epiphany tradition in Veneto. Country people would cook this cake in the embers of fires lit on the night of January 5, when they burned the *befana* or *vecia* (the effigy of the previous year) to bring good luck. This recipe is inspired by my Aunt Tali's *pinza*.

—

30 minutes preparation time
20 minutes soaking time
1 hour 5 minutes cooking time
Serves 6

150 g (5½ oz) raisins
40–60 ml (1¼–2 fl oz) *grappa* or
    eau-de-vie
500 ml (17 fl oz/2 cups) milk
fine salt
200 g (7 oz) polenta
150 g (5½ oz) raw (demerara) sugar
100 g (3½ oz) dried figs, chopped
50 g (1¾ oz/⅓ cup) pine nuts
20 g (¾ oz) fennel seeds
50 g (1¾ oz) butter, softened

50 ml (1¾ fl oz) olive oil, plus extra,
    for greasing
1 orange (preferably unwaxed)
1 lemon (preferably unwaxed)
400 g (14 oz/2⅔ cups) plain
    (all-purpose) flour
1 sachet (7 g/¼ oz) baking powder
    (preferably organic)
½ teaspoon bicarbonate of soda
    (baking soda)
50 g (1¾ oz) fresh breadcrumbs

Place the raisins in a small bowl and cover with the *grappa*, leaving for about 20 minutes to rehydrate. Meanwhile, add 150 ml (5 fl oz) of water to the milk in a saucepan and bring it to the boil over a medium heat with 2 pinches of salt. Pour in the polenta in a steady stream and cook for 5 minutes, stirring constantly. Remove from the heat.

Add the sugar, rehydrated raisins, chopped figs, pine nuts, fennel seeds, softened butter and olive oil to the saucepan. Add the finely grated zest of the orange and lemon, squeeze in the juice of the orange and then stir to combine well. Allow the mixture to cool.

Preheat the oven to 180°C (350°F). Stir the flour into the mixture, little by little, until the dough is quite firm. Add the baking powder and bicarbonate of soda, then work the dough by hand or use an electric stand mixer.

Grease a 20 cm (8 inch) square cake tin with oil and coat with the breadcrumbs. Spread out the dough in the tin to a 4 cm (1½ inch) thickness.

Bake for about 1 hour: the cake should be quite dense. Serve at room temperature, cut into small pieces.

. Cakes & festive cakes .

ITALIAN EASTER BRIOCHE
FOCACCIA PASQUALE

A Venetian yeast cake traditionally eaten at Easter time, this sweet *focaccia* is now found all year round in Venice. Unlike French brioche, it has quite a dense crumb and contains less butter and eggs. It is eaten for breakfast dipped in *caffè latte*, or as an afternoon snack, plain or spread with jam.

≡

30 minutes preparation time
2 hours 50 minutes resting time
30–40 minutes cooking time
Serves 8

20 g (¾ oz) fresh yeast or 1 sachet
  (7 g/¼ oz) dried yeast
80–100 ml (2½–3½ fl oz) lukewarm milk
600 g (1 lb 5 oz/4 cups) plain (all-purpose)
  flour, plus extra, for the cake tin
100 g (3½ oz) butter, softened
120 g (4¼ oz) sugar
1 teaspoon fine salt
finely grated zest of 1 lemon (preferably
  unwaxed)
150 ml (5 fl oz) milk
80 ml (2½ fl oz/⅓ cup) rum

4 egg yolks
30 g (1 oz) butter, melted, plus extra,
  for greasing
1 egg, beaten, for glazing

For the icing (optional)
150 g (5½ oz) icing (confectioners') sugar
1 egg white
20 ml (½ fl oz) rum
120 g (4¼ oz/¾ cup) toasted almonds,
  chopped

Combine the fresh yeast with the lukewarm milk in a mixing bowl, then add 150 g (5½ oz/1 cup) of the flour and work the mixture together briefly to combine. (If you are using dried yeast, combine it directly with the flour, then add the milk.) Cover and let this mixture rest for 20 minutes.

Cut the softened butter into small pieces and mix them into the yeast mixture. Add the sugar, salt, lemon zest, milk and rum, then the remaining flour and the egg yolks, one by one, mixing well after each addition. Knead the dough well by hand or use an electric stand mixer, cover with plastic wrap and leave to rise for 2 hours in a warm (24°C/75°F) place: the dough should double in size.

Knead the dough again for a few seconds, divide it into 16 portions and brush each portion generously with melted butter. Grease and flour a 26 cm (10½ inch) round cake tin. Shape the dough portions into balls and arrange them in the tin. Cover with plastic wrap and let the dough rise again for 30 minutes.

Preheat the oven to 180°C (350°F). Brush the balls of dough with the beaten egg. Bake for 30–40 minutes, or until the focaccia is golden brown. Remove from the tin and place on a wire rack to cool.

For the icing, if using, lightly beat the icing sugar with the egg white and rum until the mixture is smooth. Pour over the focaccia while it is still warm and scatter with the chopped almonds.

The focaccia will keep, wrapped in plastic wrap, for up to 2 days.

. Cakes & festive cakes .

VENETIAN FRIED PASTRIES
CROSTOLI VENEZIANI

Crostoli and *fritole* (next page) are fried treats eaten during Carnival in Venice and Veneto. In other parts of Italy, they are called *galani*, *cenci* or *chiacchiere*. Crostoli are made from a light and very thin dough, often cut into diamond shapes.

＝

30 minutes preparation time
1 hour resting time
15 minutes cooking time
Serves 6–8

100 g (3½ oz) raw (demerara) sugar
2 eggs
60 g (2¼ oz) butter, melted
1 small pinch salt
1 small glass (approximately 55 ml/1¾ fl oz) grappa or *eau-de-vie*
100 ml (3½ fl oz) milk
500 g (1 lb 2 oz/3⅓ cups) plain (all-purpose) flour
icing (confectioners') sugar, for dusting

For deep-frying
2 litres (70 fl oz/8 cups) peanut oil

Beat the sugar and eggs together in a mixing bowl until smooth. Add the melted butter while it's still warm, then the salt, *grappa* and milk. Add the flour gradually and work the dough until it is smooth and pliable — about 10 minutes by hand, or 5 minutes using an electric stand mixer.

Wrap the dough in plastic wrap and let it rest for 1 hour at room temperature.

On a floured work surface, roll out the dough as thinly as possible using a rolling pin, or us a pasta machine. Cut out rectangular or diamond shapes using a serrated pastry wheel.

Heat the peanut oil in a large, deep heavy-based saucepan to 180°C (350°F), or until a cube of bread dropped into the oil turns golden in 15 seconds. Deep-fry the *crostoli* in several batches, 3–4 at a time, without letting them get too brown.

Drain the *crostoli* on paper towel. Allow to cool slightly then dust with icing sugar to serve.

ITALIAN CARNIVAL FRITTERS
FRITOLE DI CARNEVALE

In Venice, it's impossible to imagine Carnival without *fritole*! In the 18th century, these deep-fried treats became Venice's official dessert. In one of his famous comedies, playwright Carlo Goldoni draws a portrait of the *fritolere*, the street vendors who made and sold *fritole* in the streets of Venice.

30 minutes preparation time
20 minutes soaking time
4 hours resting time
30 minutes cooking time
Serves 6

100 g (3½ oz) raisins
150 ml (5 fl oz) *grappa, eau-de-vie* or rum
25 g (1 oz) fresh yeast, or 1 sachet
(7 g/¼ oz) dried yeast
50 ml (1¾ fl oz) lukewarm water
1 teaspoon caster (superfine) sugar
500 g (1 lb 2 oz/3⅓ cups) plain
(all-purpose) flour
2 eggs, lightly whisked
80 g (2¾ oz) raw (demerara) sugar

½ teaspoon salt
finely grated zest of 1 lemon and 1 orange
(preferably unwaxed)
50 g (1¾ oz/⅓ cup) pine nuts
150 ml (5 fl oz) milk, if necessary
icing (confectioners') sugar, for dusting

For deep-frying
2 litres (70 fl oz/8 cups) peanut oil

Place the raisins in a small bowl and soak them in the *grappa* for 20 minutes. Dissolve the yeast in a separate cup in the lukewarm water with the caster sugar and let the mixture rest for 5 minutes. (If you are using dried yeast, combine it directly with the flour before adding the water.)

In a large bowl, use a spoon to mix the flour with the eggs, raw sugar, salt and citrus zest. Stir in the yeast mixture, pine nuts, raisins and *grappa*. Mix together well until the dough is shiny and pliable — about 10 minutes using a spoon, 5 minutes using an electric stand mixer with a paddle attachment. If the dough is too dry, add a little milk or water. Cover the dough with a cloth and let it rise for 4 hours in a warm place.

Heat the peanut oil in a large, deep heavy-based saucepan to 170°C (325°F), or until a cube of bread dropped into the oil turns golden in 20 seconds. Work the dough again for a few minutes. Using two tablespoons, shape the dough into balls the size of a large walnut.

Place a few balls in the hot oil, 4–5 at a time, and fry for about 8 minutes. When well browned, remove with a slotted spoon and drain on paper towel. Serve the *fritole* hot, dusted with icing sugar.

Oil temperature
Check the oil temperature regularly using a thermometer: it should always be between 160°C and 170°C (315°F and 325°F) so the fritole don't brown too quickly on the outside while remaining raw in the middle.

. *Cakes & festive cakes* .

CHOCOLATE & PISTACHIO CANNOLI
CANNOLI SICILIANI

It is impossible to resist the sweet delight of these famous Sicilian pastries. Originally from Palermo, the name comes from the *canna comune* ("giant cane" or "reed") once used to roll up and fry the *cannoli* dough.

=

40 minutes preparation time
15 minutes cooking time
Makes 20 cannoli

250 g (9 oz/1⅓ cup) plain (all-purpose) flour
30 g (1 oz) sugar
1 pinch salt
1 teaspoon unsweetened cocoa powder
100 ml (3½ fl oz) dry (*fine*) Marsala or
   sweet white wine
2 egg whites
30 g (1 oz) butter, melted and cooled

For deep-frying
2 litres (70 fl oz/2 cups) peanut oil

For the filling
750 g (1 lb 10 oz/3⅓ cups) ricotta
   (preferably sheep's milk)
150 g (5½ oz) icing (confectioners') sugar
1 pinch vanilla seeds
50 g (1¾ oz) candied orange peel pieces
70 g (2½ oz) dark chocolate (buttons or
   chopped)
30 g (1 oz) blanched unsalted pistachio nuts,
   chopped

P lace the flour, sugar, salt and cocoa powder in a mixing bowl. Create a well in the centre and pour in the Marsala, one egg white and the cooled melted butter. Knead for 5 minutes using an electric stand mixer, or for 10 minutes by hand, until the dough is smooth and elastic. Wrap the dough in plastic wrap and leave to rest at room temperature for 40 minutes.

Using two large bowls, push the ricotta through a sieve twice so it is smooth and creamy. Add the sifted icing sugar and the vanilla and mix together well. Chop the pieces of candied orange peel, leaving about 10 whole for decoration. Mix the chopped peel and chocolate into the ricotta. Refrigerate until required.

Take a third of the dough (leave the rest covered with plastic wrap so it doesn't dry out) and roll it out very thinly on a lightly floured work surface to a thickness of 1–2 mm (¹⁄₁₆ inch). Cut out 12 cm (4½ inch) circles, stretch them a little using your fingers and roll each circle around a *cannoli* mould. Overlap the ends and stick them together with a little egg white.

Heat the peanut oil in a large, deep heavy-based saucepan to 170°C (325°F), or until a cube of bread dropped in the oil turns golden in 20 seconds. Fry 3–4 *cannoli* at a time, turning with a slotted spoon, until golden brown. Remove the *cannoli* from the oil, carefully slide off the moulds and drain on paper towel.

Fill a piping (icing) bag fitted with a large, plain nozzle with the ricotta mixture. Fill the *cannoli* just before serving and decorate with pieces of candied orange peel and chopped pistachios.

. Cakes & festive cakes .

DOUGHNUTS WITH SOUR CHERRIES
ZEPPOLE DI SAN GIUSEPPE

In the south of Italy, *zeppole* are made for Carnival or Saint Joseph's Day (March 19).
Each region has its own version, but the most decadent are from Naples, where they're
fried or baked and then topped with crème pâtissière and sour cherries. In Sicily, the
Sfinci di San Giuseppe are served with a mixture of ricotta, candied fruit and chocolate.

40 minutes preparation time
55 minutes cooking time
Makes 10–12 *zeppole*

1 quantity crème pâtissière *(see page 151)*

For the choux pastry
1 pinch sugar
1 pinch salt
80 g (2¾ oz) butter

130 g (4¾ oz) plain (all-purpose) flour
4 eggs, lightly whisked
a few spoonfuls of *amarene*
    (sour cherries) in syrup

Make the crème pâtissière as per the recipe on page 151 then cover closely with
plastic wrap to prevent a rubbery skin from forming then refrigerate until needed.
For the choux pastry, heat 180 ml (6 fl oz) of water and the sugar in a saucepan over
a low heat. Add the salt and the butter in pieces, and stir from time to time. When the water
comes to the boil, remove from the heat and add the sifted flour all at once, mixing it in quickly.
Return the saucepan to a low heat and keep stirring vigorously for 10 minutes, or until the dough
comes away from the sides.

Transfer the dough to a mixing bowl and keep stirring with a wooden spoon or use an electric
stand mixer to cool the dough and make it more pliable. Add the eggs a little at a time to the
lukewarm mixture, still stirring by hand or using the mixer — don't add more egg until the
previous addition has been fully absorbed. In the end, the dough should be smooth, slightly
sticky and form a ribbon when it falls.

Preheat the oven to 190°C (375°F) and line a baking tray with baking paper.

Using a piping (icing) bag fitted with a fluted 1.2 cm (½ inch) nozzle, fill the bag with the choux
mixture and pipe 5 cm (2 inch) rings, letting the "tail" of the mixture fall back into the middle
of the ring. Bake for about 40 minutes, lowering the temperature to 170°C (325°F) after
10 minutes. Let the *zeppole* cool, then top with crème pâtissière and cherries.

Fried zeppole
*Make the choux pastry as indicated above but only use 40 g (1½ oz) butter. Heat some peanut
oil in a frying pan to 180°C (350°F), or until a cube of bread dropped into the oil turns golden
brown in 15 seconds.*

Pipe each zeppola *on a circle of baking paper and lower wth the paper into the hot oil — the*
zeppola *will detach from the paper. Fry for 2–3 minutes on each side, or until golden.*

Roll the zeppole *while they're still hot in 100 g (3½ oz) icing (confectioners') sugar mixed with
1 teaspoon ground cinnamon, or cool before topping with crème pâtissière and cherries.*

. *Cakes & festive cakes* .

BISCUITS,
BREAKFASTS
&
SNACKS

SOFT AMARETTI

Amaretti have been a traditional product of northern Italy since the 19th century. Whether they are soft, like the ones from Sassello in Liguria, or crunchy, like those from Saronno in Lombardy, they contain a small amount of *armelline*, the kernels found inside apricot stones, which give them their slight bitterness, hence the name *amaretti*. To make them at home, a good-quality bitter almond extract can be used instead.

20 minutes preparation time
30 minutes resting time
25 minutes cooking time
Makes 20 biscuits

200 g (7 oz/2 cups) ground almonds
100 g (3½ oz) caster (superfine) sugar
2 egg whites
2 teaspoons bitter almond extract (use according to strength)
    or 50 g (1¾ oz) ground apricot kernels
100 g (3½ oz) icing (confectioners') sugar

Combine the ground almonds with 50 g (1¾ oz) of the caster sugar. In a large bowl, whisk the egg whites with the remaining caster sugar until firm. Stir in the ground almond mixture and the almond extract to form quite a thick and sticky dough.

Pour the icing sugar in a bowl and lightly coat your hands with it. Gently roll walnut-sized balls of dough between your palms then roll them in the bowl of icing sugar until completey coated. Shake off the excess icing sugar.

Preheat the oven to 160°C (315°F). Line a baking tray with baking paper.

Meanwhile, place the biscuits on the tray, flattening them a little, and let them dry, uncovered, at room temperature for about 30 minutes.

Bake the biscuits for 25 minutes: the *amaretti* should be slightly coloured and tender in the middle. Let them cool. The *amaretti* will keep in an airtight container or a sealed bag for up to 3 weeks.

Amaretti in desserts
I like to use these amaretti to flavour my desserts: crumbled in the base of the tin for a chocolate cake (see page 66), or dipped in coffee for a tiramisù (see page 18).

VENETIAN POLENTA BISCUITS
ZALETI

This little Venetian biscuit gets its name from the yellow polenta it is made from: *gialla* (yellow) in Italian would have led to *gialletti*, then *zaleti*. In the 18th century, they were sold in the street during Carnival or served at the end of wedding feasts. Today they are found all year round in Italian *pasticceria*.

20 minutes preparation time
20 minutes soaking time
1 hour 15 minutes refrigeration time
15 minutes cooking time
Makes 20 biscuits

50 g (1¾ oz) raisins
50 ml (1¾ fl oz) *grappa* or *eau-de-vie*
125 g (4½ oz) fine polenta
125 g (4½ oz) plain (all-purpose) flour
½ teaspoon baking powder (preferably organic)
1 pinch salt
80 g (2¾ oz) butter, cold
100 g (3½ oz) sugar
1 egg
1 egg yolk
finely grated zest of 1 lemon (preferably unwaxed)
1 pinch vanilla powder

Soak the raisins in a small bowl with the *grappa* and a little added water to cover. In a large bowl, combine the polenta with the flour, baking powder and salt.

Cut the butter into small pieces. In another bowl, using your fingers, work the sugar into the butter to make a coarse, crumbly mixture, then mix in the eggs and egg yolk. Add the polenta mixture, lemon zest and vanilla. Knead lightly. Work the drained raisins through the dough then rest it in the refrigerator for at least 1 hour.

Make rolls of dough 3–5 cm (1¼–2 inches) in diameter, cut them on the diagonal every 7 cm (2¾ inches) and shape the pieces into small oval-shaped loaves. Place the biscuits on a baking tray lined with baking paper and return to the refrigerator for 15 minutes.

Preheat the oven to 170°C (325°F).

Bake for about 15 minutes, until the *zaleti* are lightly coloured. Let them cool. They will keep in an airtight container for up to 3 weeks.

. Biscuits, breakfasts & snacks .

VENETIAN RING BISCUITS
BUSSOLAI

Bussolai are delicious biscuits typical of the island of Burano, next to Venice, where they are sold loose in bakeries. You can also find "S"-shaped versions, called "esse".

20 minutes preparation time
1 hour 15 minutes refrigeration time, or overnight
15 minutes cooking time
Makes 20–30 biscuits

3 egg yolks
100 g (3½ oz) sugar
120 g (4¼ oz) butter, softened
1 pinch salt
½ vanilla bean, seeds only
finely grated zest of 1 lemon (preferably unwaxed)
250 g (9 oz/1⅔ cups) plain (all-purpose) flour
1 egg white

Whisk the egg yolks in a bowl with the sugar until the mixture has a mousse-like consistency. Add the softened butter, salt, vanilla seeds, lemon zest, then the sifted flour. Knead the dough, without overworking it, then shape it into a log. Wrap it in plastic wrap and refrigerate for at least 1 hour (or even overnight).

Cut the dough into 10 cm (4 inch) pieces. Roll into sausage shapes about 1 cm (½ inch) thick and shape them into rings by gluing the ends together with a little egg white. Arrange the biscuits on a baking tray lined with baking paper and refrigerate for 15 minutes.

Preheat the oven to 170°C (325°F).

Bake the biscuits for about 15 minutes, until they are lightly coloured. Let them cool. They will keep in an airtight container for up to 3 weeks.

Enjoy the *bussolai* at the end of a meal, dunked in a sweet wine.

ALMOND BISCOTTI
CANTUCCI

These dry biscuits from Prato, in Tuscany, are enjoyed dunked in *vin santo* (sweet wine) or coffee. Throughout Italy they are known as *cantucci* or *cantuccini*, but if you are in Tuscany, you should instead ask for *biscotti di Prato*. They have come to be known as *biscotti* internationally.

25 minutes preparation time
15 minutes refrigeratio time
1 hour cooking time
Makes about 70 biscuits

280 g (10 oz/1¾ cups) whole almonds, blanched
   or unblanched
4 eggs
380 g (13½ oz) caster (superfine) sugar
50 g (1¾ oz) butter
1 pinch fine salt
finely grated zest of 1 orange (preferably unwaxed)
500 g (1 lb 2 oz/3⅓ cups) plain (all-purpose) flour
1 teaspoon baking powder (preferably organic)
1 egg yolk, beaten
40 ml (1¼ fl oz) milk

Preheat the oven to 180°C (350°F). Toast the almonds for 15 minutes on a metal baking tray. Meanwhile, in a large bowl, beat the eggs and sugar together for 5 minutes using an electric beater.

Melt the butter with the salt and orange zest in a double boiler (or a heatproof bowl over a saucepan of hot water, making sure the hot water doesn't touch the base of the bowl). Cool the butter to lukewarm, then add to the egg mixture. Sift in the flour and baking powder then, using an electric stand mixer or beater, work the dough until smooth. Scatter the cooled almonds evenly through the dough.

Wet your hands with cold water, then make 5 logs, 3 cm (1¼ inches) in diameter. Arrange the logs on a baking tray lined with baking paper, flattening them a little but leaving plenty of space between them. Refrigerate for 15 minutes.

In a small bowl, use a fork to beat the egg yolk with the milk and brush it over the logs. Bake for 30 minutes then remove from the oven. Reduce the oven temperature to 160°C (315°F).

Cool the logs, then cut them on the diagonal into 1 cm (½ inch) thick slices. Return the slices to the cooler oven and bake for 10 minutes on each side. Don't let them get too brown or they will become tough. The biscuits will keep in an airtight container for up to 2 weeks.

. Biscuits, breakfasts & snacks .

LADYFINGER BISCUITS
SAVOIARDI

These simple, sugary biscuits are known as *savoiardi*, because of their historical Savoy connection. It's said they were created in the Middle Ages in the kitchens of the Dukes of Savoy, in honour of a visit from the King of France. The recipe spread to Piedmont, Liguria and Sardinia, former regions of the kingdom of Savoy. They are perfect for tiramisù.

25 minutes preparation time
20 minutes cooking time
Makes about 60 biscuits

6 eggs, separated, at room temperature
150 g (5½ oz) caster (superfine) sugar
150 g (5½ oz/1 cup) plain (all-purpose) flour
40 g (1½ oz/⅓ cup) icing (confectioners') sugar

Preheat the oven to 180°C (350°F), fan-forced. Meanwhile, beat the egg whites in a bowl using an electric beater. When air bubbles start to form, add half the sugar. Once the mixture has become pale and light, add the rest of the sugar, continuing to beat until you have a smooth meringue.

In a separate bowl, lightly beat the yolks and add them little by little to the meringue. Sift the flour and fold it in very gently using a spatula, turning the mixture up from the base of the bowl. Pour the mixture into a piping (icing) bag fitted with a plain 1 cm (½ inch) nozzle.

Line three baking trays with baking paper, attaching the paper to the trays with a dab of mixture. Pipe 10 cm (4 inch) lines of mixture onto each tray, leaving some space between them. Dust with half the icing sugar using a small sieve. Wait for 5 minutes and dust again with the remaining icing sugar.

Bake the fingers for about 20 minutes — do not open the oven during the first 15 minutes. Let them cool, then gently detach from the paper. Store in an airtight container for up to 2 weeks.

UGLY BUT GOOD
BRUTTI MA BUONI

These hazelnut biscuits are called *brutti ma buoni,* which literally means "ugly but good". They come from the Langhe region (Piedmont), famous for its *tonda gentile* hazelnuts, which are said to be the best in the world. Pre-cooking the dough in the saucepan, a step not included in some recipes, adds a lovely caramelised note that enhances the flavour of the toasted hazelnuts.

40 minutes preparation time
45 minutes cooking time
Makes about 20 biscuits

170 g (6 oz) hazelnuts, blanched or unblanched
2 egg whites, at room temperature
110 g (3¾ oz/½ cup) caster (superfine) sugar

Preheat the oven to 180°C (350°F), fan-forced. Put the hazelnuts on a baking tray and toast them in the oven for 20 minutes, checking them from time to time. If they are unblanched, gather them in a kitchen towel while they're still hot and rub to remove the skins. When cooled, chop the hazelnuts roughly.

Beat the egg whites in a large bowl until firm, gradually adding the sugar until you have a smooth meringue. Add the chopped hazelnuts. Pour the mixture into a heavy-based saucepan over a low heat. Cook, stirring constantly, for 10 minutes, or until the mixture caramelises.

Line a baking tray with baking paper. Using two teaspoons, place small mounds of mixture on the tray. Bake for about 15 minutes, then leave to cool. The biscuits will keep for up to 2 weeks in an airtight container, stored in a dry place.

ALMOND & HAZELNUT BISCUITS
BACI DI DAMA

Known as "lady's kisses", these little biscuits are typical of the Piedmont region, where they were created in the mid-19th century in the city of Tortona. Depending on the area, they are made using ground almonds or ground hazelnuts. Decide for yourself, but I like to use a mixture of both.

25 minutes preparation time
2 hours 20 minutes refrigeration time
20 minutes cooking time
Makes about 25 biscuits

120 g (4¼ oz) ground almonds
80 g (2¾ oz/¾ cup) ground hazelnuts
150 g (5½ oz) raw (demerara) sugar
1 pinch fine salt
180 g (6½ oz) butter, softened
1 pinch vanilla powder
200 g (7 oz/1⅓ cups) plain (all-purpose) flour
150 g (5½ oz) dark chocolate (60–70% cocoa)

Using a food processor, process the ground almonds with the ground hazelnuts, sugar and salt until the mixture is very fine.

In a large bowl, use a wooden spoon to beat the softened butter with the vanilla until very creamy. Add the almond–hazelnut mixture and the flour and briefly knead together. Form the dough into a ball, wrap in plastic wrap and refrigerate for 2 hours.

Shape the dough into small balls the size of a hazelnut and place them on a baking tray lined with baking paper. Refrigerate for a further 20 minutes.

Preheat the oven to 170°C, fan-forced (325°F). Bake for 15–20 minutes, without letting the biscuits colour too much. Remove from the oven and leave to cool.

Meanwhile, melt the chocolate in a double boiler (or a heatproof bowl over a saucepan of hot water, making sure the hot water doesn't touch the base of the bowl). Let the chocolate cool a little and use it to sandwich the biscuits together, two by two.

The *baci* will keep for up to 2 weeks in an airtight container.

FRUIT & NUT TURNOVERS
TORTELLI DOLCI

When I was little, I loved getting involved in the process of making these *tortelli* with my Aunt Vige. The flavour of the filling is similar to *savòr*, a preserve from Emilia-Romagna made from cooked fruit and reduced grape must (*saba*). You can find it in Italian grocery shops.

25 minutes preparation time
1 hour refrigeration time
20 minutes resting time
20 minutes cooking time
Makes about 20 small turnovers

For the dough
75 g (2¾ oz) butter, cold, cut into pieces
250 g (9 oz/1⅔ cups) plain
   (all-purpose) flour
1 pinch fine salt
100 g (3½ oz) sugar
1 teaspoon baking powder,
   (preferably organic)
1 egg
a few tablespoons of anise-flavoured liqueur,
   dry (*fine*) Marsala, or milk, if preferred

1 egg white and 1 egg yolk
2 tablespoons milk, for glazing

For the filling
70 g (2½ oz) prune jam.
70 g (2½ oz) orange marmalade
130 g (4¾ oz) unsweetened chestnut purée
40 g (1½ oz) candied citron or orange
40 g (1½ oz) preserved *amarene*
   (sour cherries)
130 g (4¾ oz) pitted prunes
30 g (1 oz) almonds
30 g (1 oz) pine nuts
20 g (¾ oz) walnuts
2 tablespoons honey, or 100 ml (3½ fl oz)
   saba, if available
2 tablespoons unsweetened cocoa powder

Place the cold butter in a large bowl with the flour and salt. Using your fingers, work the butter through to make a coarse, crumbly mixture. Add the sugar, baking powder, single egg and liqueur or milk to form a pliable dough. Refrigerate the dough for 1 hour.

For the filling, mix together the jam, marmalade and chestnut purée in a bowl. Dice the candied citrus fruit, *amarene* and prunes and add to the jam mixture. Using a knife, roughly chop the nuts, combine with the honey and cocoa powder then add to the filling. Set aside in the refrigerator to rest until ready to use.

Remove the dough from the refrigerator and rest for a further 20 minutes at room temperature. Roll out the dough to about a 3 mm (⅛ inch) thickness on a lightly floured work surface. Cut out circles of pastry with an 8 cm (3¼ inch) round cookie cutter.

Place a teaspoon of filling on one half of each circle, leaving a 1 cm (½ inch) border, then fold over the other half to enclose the filling. Seal the edges with a little egg white, pressing them together with your fingers. Trim excess pastry with a serrated pastry wheel.

Preheat the oven to 180°C (350°F). Place the turnovers on a baking tray lined with baking paper. Glaze by brushing them with the egg yolk mixed with the milk. Bake for 20 minutes, or until golden.

The *tortelli* will keep for 1 week in an airtight container.

. *Biscuits, breakfasts & snacks* .

APPLE STRUDEL

Originally an Austro-Hungarian dish, strudel spread to northern Italy towards the mid-19th century. Light and cinnamon-scented, it is very popular in the north-east of Italy, mainly in the Trentino–Alto Adige region where different apple varieties are grown.

40 minutes preparation time
1 hour resting time
30 minutes cooking time
Serves 8–10

For the pastry
250 g (9 oz/1⅔ cups) plain
    (all-purpose) flour
1 egg
1 tablespoon sugar
50 ml (1¾ fl oz) water
30 g (1 oz) butter, softened

For the filling
1 kg (2 lb 4 oz) cooking apples, such
    as granny smith or reinette
60 g (2¼ oz) sugar
100 g (3½ oz) raisins

60 g (2¼ oz) pine nuts
finely grated zest of 1 lemon and 1 orange
    (preferably unwaxed)
½ teaspoon ground cinnamon
4 cloves
30 g (1 oz/½ cup) fresh breadcrumbs
1 knob butter

1 egg white, whisked
1 tablespoon sugar
20 g (¾ oz) butter, melted

Make the pastry: pour the flour into a mixing bowl, make a well and mix in the other ingredients. Knead the dough for 10 minutes until it is smooth and elastic. Wrap the dough in plastic wrap and let it rest for 30 minutes in a barely heated (30°C/85°F) oven.

For the filling, peel, core and chop the apples and place them in a mixing bowl. Add the sugar, washed raisins, pine nuts, citrus zests and spices and combine well. Let the mixture stand for about 30 minutes, mixing from time to time, then remove the cloves.

Preheat the oven to 170°C (325°F).

In a small frying pan, gently fry the breadcrumbs in the butter over a low heat until golden. Roll out the pastry dough to a 2–3 mm (¹⁄₁₆–⅛ inch) thickness then cut out three squares. Sprinkle half of each square with breadcrumbs and place a third of the apple mixture on top (leave a border at the top and bottom).

Cut out the other side of the pastry square as per the photo opposite so you have a flap to fold over. Fold the borders over the strudel, then fold over the flap, sealing it underneath the strudel. Seal the edges with some egg white. Use the pastry offcuts to make decorations to place on top of the strudels. Glaze with the remaining egg white mixed with sugar.

Arrange the strudels on a baking tray lined with baking paper. Bake for about 30 minutes. Halfway through the cooking time, brush with melted butter and continue baking until the pastry is golden.

FRIED RAVIOLI WITH RICOTTA

These ravioli are a speciality of the south of Italy, made for celebrations and Carnival. I have tasted several versions, from Sicily to Apulia. They are very decadent when deep-fried, but you can also bake them in the oven.

40 minutes preparation time
1 hour resting time
15 minutes cooking time
Makes about 20 small ravioli

For the pastry
250 g (9 oz/1⅔ cups) plain (all-purpose) flour
60 g (2¼ oz) sugar
1 pinch fine salt
50 g (1¾ oz) butter, softened
100 ml (3½ fl oz) water

1 egg white, whisked

For the filling
60 g (2¼ oz) dark chocolate (60–70% cocoa)
250 g (9 oz) ricotta
40 g (1½ oz) sugar

1 litre (35 fl oz/4 cups) peanut oil, for deep-frying
2 tablespoons icing (confectioners') sugar, for dusting

Combine the flour, sugar and salt in a large bowl, then incorporate the butter, cut into small pieces. Add water as you need it, a little at a time, and knead until you have a smooth and elastic dough. Wrap the dough in plastic wrap and let it rest for 1 hour at room temperature.

For the filling, finely chop the chocolate with a knife. Push the ricotta through a sieve into a bowl and mix to make it smooth and creamy. Mix in the sugar and chocolate.

Roll out the dough on a lightly floured surface to a 3 mm (⅛ inch) thickness. Cut out circles 10–12 cm (4–4½ inches) in diameter. Place a tablespoonful of filling on one side of each circle, then close the ravioli, sealing the edges with the egg white.

In a large, heavy-based deep saucepan, heat the peanut oil to 180°C (350°F), or until a cube of bread dropped into the oil turns golden in 15 seconds. Fry 3–4 ravioli at a time for 2–3 minutes, or until golden brown. Drain on paper towels dust with the icing sugar and serve immediately.

Variation with honey and almonds
A different filling can be made with 250 g (9 oz) ricotta, 40 g (1½ oz) honey, 30 g (1 oz) chopped almonds and the finely grated zest of 1 orange or 1 lemon (preferably unwaxed).

. *Biscuits, breakfasts & snacks* .

CHESTNUT CAKE
CASTAGNACCIO

Made from chestnut flour, this cake is typical of the regions of Tuscany,
Liguria and Emilia-Romagna, where chestnuts were a staple food
for peasants. I like to make this cake during the cold season, as it's
a bit like an energy bar! Children also enjoy it as a snack.

15 minutes preparation time
1 hour resting time
20–30 minutes cooking time
Serves 6

50 g (1¾ oz) small raisins
250 g (9 oz) chestnut flour
1 pinch fine salt
30 g (1 oz) sugar
450 ml (16 fl oz) water
80 ml (2½ oz/⅓ cup) olive oil
2 tablespoons fresh breadcrumbs
40 g (1½ oz/¼ cup) pine nuts
3–4 rosemary sprigs, chopped

Soak the raisins in a bowl of lukewarm water. Sift the chestnut flour into a
mixing bowl, add the salt and sugar. Add the water in a thin stream with
2 tablespoons of the olive oil, whisking at the same time, until the mixture
is runny. Cover the bowl with a cloth and rest at room temperature for 1 hour.

Preheat the oven to 190°C (375°F).

Grease a large tart tin or a deep baking dish (not too thick so the heat conducts
well) with 1 tablespoon of the olive oil and sprinkle with the breadcrumbs. Whisk
the batter before pouring it into the tin to a maximum depth of 1.5 cm (⅝ inch).
Pour over the remaining oil in a thin stream and mix into the batter with a spoon.

In a small frying pan, fry the pine nuts over medium heat until golden. Scatter
them over the batter with the drained raisins and rosemary. Bake for 20–30
minutes — when ready, the top should be cracked.

Serve warm or at room temperature. The *castagnaccio* will keep for 1 week in an
airtight container.

CHOC-HAZELNUT SPREAD
GIANDUJA

Gianduja was created in Turin in the mid-19th century as a form of chocolate with less cocoa. The Continental Blockade put in place by Napoleon made imported cocoa very expensive, so cheaper local Piedmontese hazelnuts make up half of the spread.

20 minutes preparation time
Makes 1 large jam jar

50 g (1¾ oz) milk chocolate
50 g (1¾ oz) dark chocolate
50 ml (1¾ fl oz) grapeseed oil or other
   neutral oil, such as sunflower
10 g (¼ oz) unsweetened cocoa powder
100 g (3½ oz) unsweetened hazelnut butter

Melt the two chocolates together in a double boiler (or a heatproof bowl over a saucepan of hot water, making sure the hot water doesn't touch the base of the bowl).

In a large bowl, whisk the oil with the sifted cocoa powder. Add the hazelnut butter, then the melted chocolates.

Pour the mixture into a large baking dish and stir constantly, spreading it out, to lower the temperature to 26–27°C (79–80.5°F).

Fill a sterilised jam jar with the mixture while it is still runny and let it rest for at least 24 hours to reach the right consistency. Store at room temperature for up to 1 month.

Hazelnut butter
You can buy pure unsweetened hazelnut butter in health food shops. If you can't find it, you can make it yourself using an electric coffee grinder or a juicer with a grinder function. For a unique flavour, choose Piedmont hazelnuts, already blanched and toasted, sold in gourmet food shops or online.

Variation
Replace the two chocolates with 100 g (3½ fl oz) milk chocolate. Children will love it!

ICE CREAMS & FROZEN DESSERTS

SABAYON & NOUGAT SEMIFREDDO

I love this frozen dessert, based on a mixture of sabayon and whipped cream combined with chocolate and *mandorlato*. The chocolate–*amaretti* version is also delicious. While there are locally made crunchy nougats, try seeking out the *mandorlato di Cologna Veneta*, made in Veneto from almonds, honey and egg whites.

50 minutes preparation time
12 hours freezing time
Serves 8

200 g (7 oz) *mandorlato* (crunchy nougat)
120 g (4¼ oz) dark chocolate (60–70% cocoa)
1 quantity sabayon *(see page 153)* with an extra 55 ml
   (1¾ fl oz) dry *(fine)* Marsala
500 ml (17 fl oz/2 cups) thickened (whipping) cream, chilled
1 teaspoon vanilla extract
1 tablespoon caster (superfine) sugar

Roughly chop the nougat. Do the same with 80 g (2¾ oz) of the dark chocolate. In a bowl, combine 150 g (5½ oz) of the nougat with the chopped chocolate and set aside the remaining nougat for decoration.

Make the sabayon according to the recipe on page 153 (adding the extra Marsala to the mixture). In a separate bowl, whip the cream with the vanilla and sugar until fairly stiff, then incorporate this chantilly cream into the cooled sabayon.

Line the base and sides of a loaf (bar) tin with plastic wrap. Spread a third of the chopped nougat–chocolate mixture in the base of the tin and cover with a layer of sabayon–whipped cream mixture. Repeat this process and finish with the nougat–chocolate mixture. Place the semifreddo in the freezer overnight.

Melt the remaining chocolate in a double boiler (or a heatproof bowl over a saucepan of hot water, making sure the hot water doesn't touch the base of the bowl), or microwave on low in a heatproof bowl. Spread it out thinly on a light metal baking tray, chilled (place in the freezer for 30 minutes before this step).

Once the chocolate starts to set but before it is completely solid, scrape it with the smooth blade of a knife to make thin shavings.

Before serving, leave the semifreddo at room temperature for 10–15 minutes. Unmould it on to a plate and remove the plastic wrap. Decorate with the rest of the chopped nougat and the chocolate shavings.

Variation
Replace the nougat with pieces of amaretti.

. *Ice creams & frozen desserts* .

GRANITAS

25 minutes preparation time
30 minutes resting time
3 hours 30 minutes freezing time
Serves 6

Coffee

300 ml (10½ fl oz) sparkling mineral water
150 g (5½ oz) raw (demerara) sugar
700 ml (24 fl oz) strong espresso coffee
200 ml (7 fl oz) thin (pouring) cream
1 tablespoon icing (confectioners') sugar

Heat the water and sugar in a saucepan over a high heat and bring to the boil for a few minutes. Let this syrup cool, then add the coffee. Pour the room-temperature mixture into a wide and shallow container and let it set in the freezer for 90 minutes.

Scrape the frozen surface with a fork to flake the ice, then return to the freezer. Repeat this process two or three times, every 40 minutes.

In a bowl, whip the cream with the icing sugar. Serve the granita in large glasses or dessert bowls, with whipped cream on the side.

Lemon

750 ml (26 fl oz) sparkling mineral water
140 g (5 oz/⅔ cup) raw (demerara) sugar
peeled zest of 1 lemon (preferably unwaxed)
250 ml (9 fl oz/1 cup) juice from good-quality lemons

Heat the water, sugar and lemon peel in a saucepan over a high heat and bring to the boil for a few minutes. Let the syrup infuse for 30 minutes, then remove the peel. Add the lemon juice. Pour the room-temperature mixture into a wide and shallow container, and let it set in the freezer for 90 minutes.

Scrape the frozen surface with a fork to flake the ice, then return to the freezer. Repeat this process two or three times, every 40 minutes. Serve the granita in large glasses or dessert bowls.

Almond

200 ml (7 fl oz) sparkling mineral water
90 g (3¼ oz) raw (demerara) sugar
1 litre (35 fl oz/4 cups) unsweetened almond milk
40 ml (1¼ fl oz) bitter almond extract

Heat the water and sugar in a saucepan over a high heat for a few minutes. Let this syrup cool. Add the almond milk and bitter almond extract. Pour the room-temperature mixture into a wide and shallow container, and let it set in the freezer for 90 minutes.

Scrape the frozen surface with a fork to flake the ice, then return to the freezer. Repeat this process two or three times, every 40 minutes. Serve the granita in large glasses or dessert bowls.

VANILLA ICE CREAM

The recipe for ice cream is said to be the work of Bernardo Buontalenti, serving at the Medici court in Florence at the end of the 16th century. He combined snow with milk and eggs, flavoured with lemon, and put everything into a machine of his own invention. It's the milk and egg yolks that make ice cream so creamy!

50 minutes preparation time
10 minutes cooking time
6 hours refrigeration time, or overnight
Serves 6

350 ml (12 fl oz) milk
150 ml (5 fl oz) thin (pouring) cream
1 tablespoon acacia honey
1 vanilla bean, split lengthways and seeds scraped
4 egg yolks
120 g (4¼ oz) raw (demerara) sugar
10 g (¼ oz) cornflour (cornstarch), sifted
10 g (¼ oz) semi-skimmed powdered milk

Heat the milk, cream, honey and vanilla bean and its seeds in a saucepan over a low heat. Beat the egg yolks with the sugar in a mixing bowl and add the cornflour. Pour a third of the warm milk over the yolks, whisking quickly. Pour this mixture back into the saucepan and add the powdered milk. Stir until the custard coats the spoon — make sure it doesn't boil.

Transfer the custard to a mixing bowl placed over a container of iced water to cool it down quickly. Place the custard in the refrigerator for at least 6 hours (or even overnight).

Remove the vanilla bean and blend the cold custard with a hand-held blender to produce a smooth consistency. Pour the mixture into an ice cream maker and churn for 20–30 minutes. Serve the ice cream immediately or after a few hours resting in the freezer in a well-sealed plastic container.

Affogato
With this great home-made classic, you can make an affogato: a scoop of vanilla ice cream dropped in an espresso coffee — a true delight!

The key ingredients for creamy ice creams
Use honey (as in this recipe) instead of glucose and invert sugar, and replace the usual thickeners of shop-bought ice creams with powdered milk and cornflour. This way your ice cream will have a smooth and creamy texture and won't harden too much in the freezer.

Stracciatella

CHOC–VANILLA ICE CREAM

120 g (4¼ oz) raw (demerara) sugar
10 g (¼ oz) cornflour (cornstarch), sifted
20 g (¾ oz) semi-skimmed powdered milk
300 ml (10½ fl oz) milk
200 ml (7 fl oz) thin (pouring) cream
1 tablespoon acacia honey
1 vanilla bean, split lengthways and seeds scraped
80 g (2¾ oz) dark chocolate (60–70% cocoa)

Combine the sugar in a bowl with the cornflour and powdered milk. In a saucepan, heat the milk, cream, honey and vanilla bean and its seeds over a low heat. Once the mixture is lukewarm, remove the vanilla bean and pour in the sugar mixture in a stream. Bring to just under the boil, whisking constantly, then turn off the heat.

Transfer the mixture to a mixing bowl placed over a container of iced water to cool it down quickly. Refrigerate for 6 hours, or overnight.

Finely chop the dark chocolate with a knife. Stir the chilled mixture and pour it into an ice-cream maker to churn for 20–30 minutes.

Add the chopped chocolate in two or three batches, and churn for another minute.

Serve the ice cream immediately, or after a few hours in the freezer in a well-sealed plastic container.

50 minutes preparation time • 10 minutes cooking time • 6 hours refrigeration time, or overnight • Makes about 800 ml (28 fl oz)

. *Ice creams & frozen desserts* .

PISTACHIO ICE CREAM

350 ml (12 fl oz) milk
150 ml (5 fl oz) thin (pouring) cream
1 tablespoon acacia honey
4 egg yolks
110 g (3¾ oz/½ cup) raw (demerara) sugar
10 g (¼ oz) cornflour (cornstarch), sifted
10 g (¼ oz) semi-skimmed powdered milk
70 g (2½ oz) unsweetened pistachio paste
1 teaspoon bitter almond extract

Heat the milk, cream and honey in a saucepan over a low heat. In a bowl, beat the egg yolks with the sugar and add the cornflour. Pour a third of the warm milk over the yolk mixture, whisking quickly. Return this mixture to the saucepan and add the powdered milk. Stir until the custard coats a spoon (make sure it doesn't boil).

Pour the custard into a mixing bowl and add the pistachio paste and bitter almond extract. Blend the mixture in a food processor until creamy.

Return the mixture to the bowl and set it over a container of iced water to cool it down quickly. Refrigerate for 6 hours, or overnight.

Blend the chilled mixture in the processor again, then pour into an ice-cream maker. Churn for 20–30 minutes.

Serve the ice cream immediately, or after a few hours in the freezer in a well-sealed plastic container.

50 minutes preparation time • 10 minutes cooking time • 6 hours refrigeration time, or overnight • Makes about 700 ml (24 fl oz)

. Ice creams & frozen desserts .

Gianduja

CHOC–HAZELNUT ICE CREAM

350 ml (12 fl oz) milk
150 ml (5 fl oz) thin (pouring) cream
1 tablespoon acacia honey
4 egg yolks
120 g (4¼ oz) raw (demerara) sugar
10 g (¼ oz) cornflour (cornstarch), sifted
60 g (2¼ oz) dark chocolate (70% cocoa)
10 g (¼ oz) semi-skimmed powdered milk
60 g (2¼ oz) unsweetened hazelnut butter

Heat the milk, cream and honey in a saucepan over a low heat. In a bowl, beat the egg yolks with the sugar and add the cornflour. Pour a third of the warm milk over the yolk mixture, whisking quickly. Return this to the saucepan and add the powdered milk. Stir until the custard coats a spoon (make sure it doesn't boil).

Roughly chop the dark chocolate with a knife. Pour the warm custard into a mixing bowl, add the hazelnut paste and chocolate. Blend in a food processor until creamy. Return the mixture to the bowl and set it over a container of iced water to cool it quickly. Refrigerate for 6 hours, or overnight.

Blend the chilled mixture again, then pour it into an ice-cream maker and churn for 20–30 minutes.

Serve the ice cream immediately, or after a few hours in the freezer in a well-sealed plastic container.

50 minutes preparation time • 10 minutes cooking time • 6 hours refrigeration time, or overnight • Makes about 700 ml (24 fl oz)

COFFEE
ICE CREAM

350 ml (12 fl oz) milk
150 ml (5 fl oz) thin (pouring) cream
1 tablespoon acacia honey
peeled zest of 1 lemon
4 egg yolks
140 g (5 oz/⅔ cup) raw (demerara) sugar
10 g (¼ oz) cornflour (cornstarch), sifted
10 g (¼ oz) semi-skimmed powdered milk
3 heaped tablespoons instant coffee

Heat the milk, cream, honey and lemon zest in a saucepan over a low heat. In a bowl, beat the egg yolks with the sugar and add the cornflour. Pour a third of the warm milk over the yolk mixture, whisking quickly. Return this mixture to the saucepan and add the powdered milk. Stir on a low heat until the custard coats a spoon (make sure it doesn't boil).

Pour the warm custard into a mixing bowl and add the instant coffee. Remove the lemon zest and blend in a food processor until smooth. Place the bowl over a container of iced water to cool the custard down quickly. Refrigerate for 6 hours, or overnight.

Blend the chilled mixture again before pouring it into an ice-cream maker. Churn for 20–30 minutes.

Serve the ice cream immediately, or after a few hours in the freezer in a well-sealed plastic container.

50 minutes preparation time •10 minutes cooking time • 6 hours refrigeration time, or overnight • Makes about 700 ml (24 fl oz)

. Ice creams & frozen desserts .

SORBETS

Raspberry

25 minutes preparation time
1 hour 30 minutes refrigeration time
Serves 4

250 g (9 oz/2 cups) fresh raspberries
20 ml (½ fl oz) lemon juice
60 ml (2 fl oz/¼ cup) sparkling mineral water
80 g (2¾ oz) raw (demerara) sugar
1 tablespoon acacia honey

Wash the fresh raspberries, blend them in a food processor and then strain to filter out the seeds. Sprinkle with the lemon juice.

Bring the water and sugar to the boil in a saucepan over a high heat for a few minutes until a syrup is formed, then add the honey and combine. Allow to cool. Mix the syrup with the raspberry purée. Set aside in the refrigerator for at least 1 hour.

Pour the mixture into an ice-cream maker and churn for 30 minutes. Serve the sorbet immediately, or after a few hours in the freezer in a well sealed plastic container.

Sundaes
In glass serving bowls, layer some lightly sweetened whipped cream — 400 ml (14 fl oz) thickened (whipping) cream whipped with 2 tablespoons icing (confectioners') sugar — a roughly crumbled amaretto biscuit and a few preserved amarene (sour cherries) with their syrup. Finish with a quenelle of raspberry sorbet on top. Makes 4–6 sundaes.

Lemon

25 minutes preparation time
1 hour 30 minutes refrigeration time
Serves 4

250 ml (9 fl oz/1 cup) sparkling mineral water
110 g (3¾ oz/½ cup) raw (demerara) sugar
1 tablespoon acacia honey
150 ml (5 fl oz) juice from good-quality lemons (about 5 lemons)
finely grated zest of ½ lemon

Bring the water and sugar to the boil in a saucepan over a high heat for a few minutes until a syrup is formed, then add the honey and combine. Cool, then add the lemon juice and zest. Refrigerate for at least 1 hour.

Pour the mixture into an ice-cream maker and churn for 30 minutes. Serve the sorbet immediately, or after a few hours in the freezer in a well-sealed plastic container.

. Ice creams & frozen desserts .

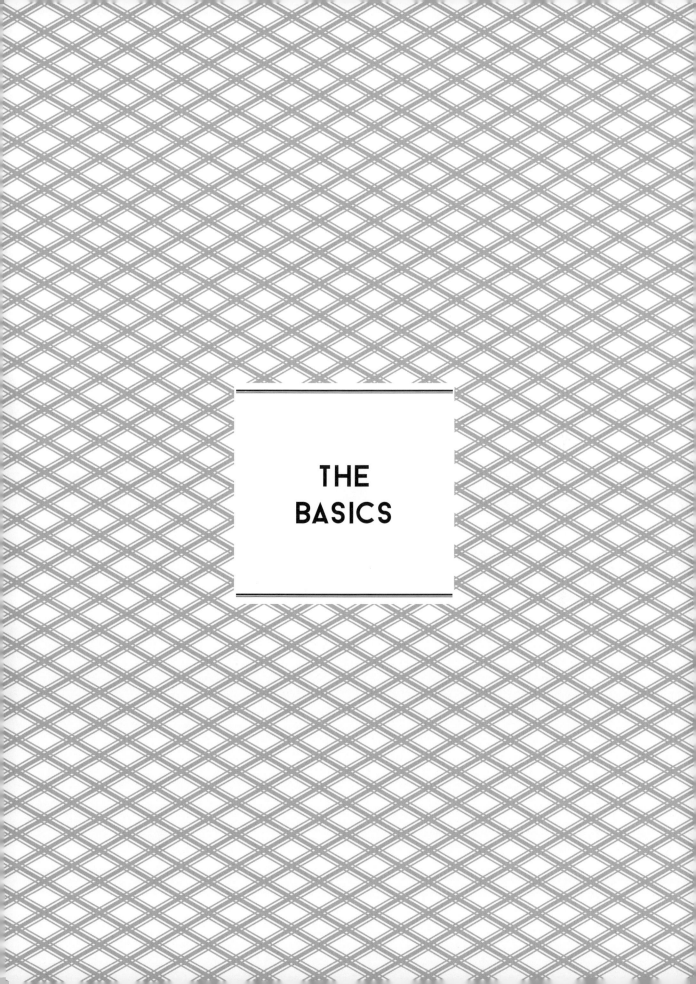

THE
BASICS

SHORTCRUST PASTRY

10 minutes preparation time
3 hours resting time
25 minutes cooking time
For a 24 cm (9½ inch) tart tin
    or 6 or 7 tartlet tins

250 g (9 oz/1⅔ cups) plain
    (all-purpose) flour
1 pinch salt
80 g (2¾ oz) raw (demerara)
    sugar
120 g (4¼ oz) butter, well chilled,
    plus extra, for greasing
finely grated zest of 1 lemon
    (preferably unwaxed)
1 egg

In a large bowl, mix 1 tablespoon of the flour with the salt, sugar and diced butter until you have a coarse, crumbly mixture. Incorporate the zest, egg and remaining flour. Don't overwork the dough.

Shape into a flattened round, wrap the dough in plastic wrap and refrigerate for 2 hours.

Take the dough out of the refrigerator and, after 30 minutes at room temperature, roll it out on a lightly floured work surface. Don't handle the pastry too much, so it stays cold.

Grease the tart tin and line it with the pastry dough. Press gently with your fingers and trim the overhanging edges. Prick the base with a fork.

Set aside in the refrigerator for 30 minutes before cooking according to the recipe you are using.

Variation: Linzer pastry, typical of the Trentino–Alto Adige region

Without changing the method, use 180 g (6½ oz) butter, 50 g (1¾ oz) sugar and 2 egg yolks instead of the quantities listed above.

Add 1 teaspoon ground cinnamon, 40 g (1½ oz) ground hazelnuts and 1 pinch baking powder, preferably organic.

This pastry is perfect for a berry jam tart.

GENOISE/PAN DI SPAGNA

20 minutes preparation time
35 minutes cooking time
Serves 6–8

butter, for greasing
6 eggs, at room temperature
160 g (5¾ oz) raw (demerara)
    sugar
160 g (5¾ oz) plain (all- purpose)
    flour, plus extra, for the cake tin
1 pinch salt

Preheat the oven to 180°C (350°F). Butter and flour a 24 cm (9½ inch) round cake tin (or 20–22 cm/ 8–8½ inch tin for a taller cake).

Using an electric beater or an electric stand mixer, beat the eggs with the sugar for 10 minutes: the mixture should be very light and mousse-like and triple in volume. Gently fold in the sifted flour and salt with a spatula, turning the mixture up from the base so you keep the air in the mixture.

Pour the batter into the tin and bake for 35 minutes — don't open the oven during the cooking time.

Turn out the hot genoise onto a wire rack. Allow it to cool completely before filling.

Storage
You can freeze the genoise without any problem.

This "Spanish bread" was created by an Italian pastry chef during his time with the Spanish royal family in the middle of the 18th century. This cake can be used instead of ladyfinger biscuits in tiramisù and works wonders in the Zuppa inglese (see page 24) and My Birthday Cake (see page 86)!

. The basics .

CRÈME ANGLAISE

20 minutes preparation time
20 minutes resting time
10 minutes cooking time
Serves 6

500 ml (17 fl oz/2 cups) milk
1 vanilla bean, split lengthways
    and seeds scraped
4 egg yolks, at room
    temperature
80 g (2¾ oz) raw (demerara)
    sugar

Heat the milk in a saucepan over a low heat with the vanilla bean and its seeds until the milk begins to simmer. Remove from the heat and let the milk infuse, covered, for 20 minutes. Remove the vanilla bean and reheat the milk on a low heat.

Beat the egg yolks and sugar in a mixing bowl until the mixture is pale and light. Still whisking, pour the warm milk over the eggs.

Pour this mixture into a saucepan and thicken over a very low heat, stirring constantly with a wooden spoon. Do not let it boil. Test the consistency by coating a spoon with the custard and running a finger through it: if it leaves a clean trace, the custard is ready.

Cool the custard by pouring into a bowl set over a container of iced water, stirring regularly. Eat within 12 hours.

CRÈME PÂTISSIÈRE

20 minutes preparation time
30 minutes resting time
15 minutes cooking time
Serves 6

500 ml (17 fl oz/2 cups) milk
peeled zest of 1 lemon and/or
   1 vanilla bean, split
   lengthways and seeds
   scraped
4 egg yolks, at room
   temperature
100 g (3½ oz) raw (demerara)
   sugar
50 g (1¾ oz/⅓ cup) plain
   (all-purpose) flour, sifted

Heat the milk in a saucepan over a low heat with the lemon zest and/or the vanilla bean and its seeds until the milk begins to simmer. Take off the heat and let the milk infuse, covered, for 30 minutes.

Remove the zest and/or the vanilla bean and reheat the milk over a low heat. Beat the egg yolks with the sugar in a mixing bowl. Whisk in the flour, then the warm milk, little by little.

Pour the mixture into a saucepan and thicken over a low heat, stirring constantly. Allow 1–2 minutes from when the mixture comes to the boil, then pour the crème into a baking dish or mixing bowl. Cover immediately with plastic wrap, with the wrap in contact with the surface of the crème so it doesn't form a skin.

Let the crème cool completely, then refrigerate. Whisk the crème to loosen it before using.

MASCARPONE CREAM

20 minutes preparation time
Serves 6

250 g (9 oz) mascarpone
    cheese
60 g (2¼ oz/½ cup) icing
    (confectioners') sugar
seeds of 1 vanilla bean
200 ml (7 fl oz) thin (pouring)
    cream, well chilled

In a mixing bowl, beat the mascarpone with the
sifted icing sugar and vanilla seeds, using a wooden
spoon, until smooth.

Add the cream, little by little, mixing in with
a whisk.

Set aside in the refrigerator until serving time.

SABAYON

15 minutes preparation time
10 minutes cooking time
Serves 6

6 egg yolks, at room
   temperature
100 g (3½ oz) sugar
150 ml (5 fl oz) dry (*fine*)
   Marsala

Combine the egg yolks, sugar and Marsala in
a heatproof bowl. Heat this mixture over a saucepan
of simmering water (be careful, the water mustn't
boil and the base of the bowl should not touch the
water), beating with an electric beater for about
10 minutes, or until the mixture forms a light mousse.

To cool the sabayon, dip the base of the bowl in
a container of iced water and stir the mixture gently
and regularly.

A few serving suggestions:
The sabayon can be served at any temperature,
depending on the recipe: warm with biscuits,
ice cream or fresh fruit; cold, mixed with whipped
cream to make a semifreddo (see page 134), or
to fill a genoise or pandoro (see page 90).

. *The basics* .

CITRUS FRUITS

1. Sicilian orange marmalade • 2. Sicilian honey • 3. *Babà* in *limoncello* • 4. *Amarene* (sour cherries) in syrup • 5. *Mostarda*: candied fruit, whole or puréed, with mustard oil • 6. Orange flower water • 7. Rosewater • 8. *Limoncello* from Sorrento: liqueur made from lemon zest, typical of the Campania coast • 9. Candied citrus peel: the best is sold in segments or large pieces (less dry), to be cut up at home • 10. Lemons and oranges: buy organic or unwaxed ones when using the zest

11

14

11

15

18

16

12   13   17

ALMONDS

11. Crunchy *amaretti* (large and mini) • 12. *Amaretto* liqueur: naturally flavoured with almonds and bitter almonds •
13. Bitter almond extract: choose natural bitter almond flavour, extract or essential oil (organic, use in drops) • 14.
Crunchy *mandorlato* from *Cologna Veneta*: a typical Veneto nougat, full of almonds and honey • 15. *Amaretti
morbidi*: soft *amaretti* • 16. Marzipan: paste made from ground blanched almonds and sugar • 17. Almonds: the
best are from Avola in Sicily • 18. *Torrone di mandorle*: crunchy nougat with caramelised almonds

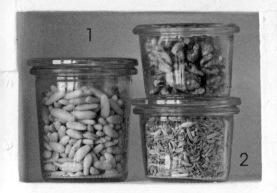

⊙THER NUTS & DRIED FRUITS

1. Nuts: pine nuts, walnuts, pistachios, hazelnuts • 2. *Semi di finocchio*: fennel seeds • 3. Dried fruit: raisins, figs • 4. *Nocciolini di Chivasso*: mini Piedmontese hazelnut amaretti • 5. *Torrone di pistacchio*: pistachio nougat • 6. Pistachio paste and ground pistachio nuts, typical of Bronte in Sicily • 7. *Gianduja* paste and *gianduiotti*, typical of Piedmont • 8. *Cioccolato di Modica* (Sicily): artisanal Sicilian chocolate. Its grainy texture is due to cold-processing • 9. *Panforte*: a traditional Christmas cake from Siena, made from dried fruit and nuts • 10. *I marroni canditi*: candied chestnuts

14

11

12

13

15

16

17

18

19

LIQUEURS, SUGARS & FLOURS

11. *Marsala*: Sicilian fortified wine, varying according to grape type, age and sweetness. Use *Marsala fine* for biscuits and desserts • 12. *Saba*: grape must syrup from the Emilia-Romagna region • 13. *Alchermes*: bright-red liqueur made from spices, rose and orange flower water, typical of Florence • 14. *Liquirizia*: pure licorice from Calabria • 15. *Zucchero di canna biondo*: organic raw (demerara) sugar • 16. *Caffè*: Italian espresso coffee • 17. *Grappa*: *eau-de-vie* made from grape pomace • 18. Artisanal *pandoro* and *panettone* • 19. Organic wheat flour and polenta (fine cornmeal)

RECIPE INDEX

ACKNOWLEDGMENTS

Grazie, grazie, grazie to the whole *Dolce* team!

To Akiko Ida for his *bellissime* photographs, to Sabrina Fauda-Role for the magic styling accessories she finds, to my assistant Annalisa Papagna, a great *dolci* enthusiast, for her precious assistance, and to the Marabout team who entrusted me with this decadent project.

Grazie mille to Emmanuelle Mourareau for his help and friendship, to Francesca Solarino, to all of my Italian friends who inspired me with their recipes, in particular Manuela Dorpetti and Anna D'Alessandro.

To my whole family who passed on their enjoyment of good things.

To Eva and Philippe for their support and… sweet tooths.

To Alessandra Pierini from the Rap food store in Paris, Anna Chierici from Qualitalia and Filippo Giarolo, who select the best Italian products!

Grazie to Kenwood for the mixers and accessories and to De' Longhi for the ice-cream maker.

BIBLIOGRAPHY

For the recipes

Artusi P., *La scienza in cucina e l'arte di mangiar bene*, L'Arte della Stampa, 1891, Newton Compton, Rome, 1989

Bay A., Salvatori P., *La cucina nazionale italiana*, Adriano Salani Editore (Ponte alle Grazie), Milan, 2008

Collectif, *La cucina delle festività religiose*, Accademia Italiana della cucina, Milan, 2010

Collectif, *L'Italia dei dolci*, Slowfood Editore, Bra (Cuneo), 2003

Collectif, *L'Italia dei dolci*, Touring Editore, Milan, 2004

Guarnaschelli Gotti M., *Grande enciclopedia illustrata della gastronomia*, Arnoldo Mondadori Editore, Milan, 2007

Montersino L., *Tiramisù e chantilly*, Fabbri Editori, Milan, 2007

Scappi B., *Opera*, Tramezzino Editore, Venezia 1570, Arnaldo Forni Editore, 1981

Vissani G., *L'altro Vissani – Dolce come pochi*, Rai Eri, Rome, 2012

For the introduction

Capatti A., Montanari M., *La cucina italiana: storia di una cultura*, editori Laterza, Roma-Bari, 1999

De Medici Stucchi L., *Il grande libro dei dolci*, Mondadori, Milano, 1988

Dickie J., *Delizia! Une histoire culinaire de l'Italie*, Buchet/Chastel, Paris, 2009

Montanari M., *Il cibo come cultura*, editori Laterza, Roma-Bari, 2004

Montanari M., *L'identità italiana in cucina*, editori Laterza, Roma-Bari, 2010

Published in 2016 by Murdoch Books, an imprint of Allen & Unwin
First published by Hachette Livre (Marabout) in 2014

Murdoch Books Australia
83 Alexander Street
Crows Nest NSW 2065
Phone: +61 (0) 2 8425 0100
Fax: +61 (0) 2 9906 2218
murdochbooks.com.au
info@murdochbooks.com.au

Murdoch Books UK
Erico House, 6th Floor
93–99 Upper Richmond Road
Putney, London SW15 2TG
Phone: +44 (0) 20 8785 5995
murdochbooks.co.uk
info@murdochbooks.co.uk

For Corporate Orders & Custom Publishing contact
Noel Hammond, National Business Development Manager, Murdoch Books Australia

Publisher: Corinne Roberts
Designer: Collectifa3
Layout: Transparence
Photographer: Akiko Ida
Stylist: Sabrina Fauda-Role
Translator: Melissa McMahon
Editor: Karen Lateo
Editorial Managers: Barbara McClenahan & Katie Bosher
Production Manager: Mary Bjelobrk

A cataloguing-in-publication entry is available from the catalogue of the National Library of Australia at nla.gov.au.

ISBN 978 1 74336 622 6 Australia
ISBN 978 1 74336 739 1 UK

A catalogue record for this book is available from the British Library.

Colour reproduction by Splitting Image Colour Studio Pty Ltd, Clayton, Victoria
Printed by 1010 Printing International Limited, China

IMPORTANT: Those who might be at risk from the effects of salmonella poisoning (the elderly, pregnant women, young children and those suffering from immune deficiency diseases) should consult their doctor with any concerns about eating raw eggs.

OVEN GUIDE: You may find cooking times vary depending on the oven you are using. For fan-forced ovens, as a general rule, set the oven temperature to 20°C (35°F) lower than indicated in the recipe.